Sacred
PATH TO
WELLNESS

CREATING MIRACLES IN OUR SOUL
AND BODY THROUGH
NON-TRADITIONAL METHODS

JOY ANDREASEN

ISBN 978-0-9898771-4-5

Disclaimer

I am not a doctor or licensed professional. The techniques described in this book are not a substitute for professional or medical treatment or advice. This information is presented to be a tool for enhancing your spiritual, physical, mental and emotional well-being and should be used in tandem with professional treatment.

In Virginia where I live, I am required to have a "fortune teller's license" to practice these techniques and I have complied with the law. I hold no responsibility for the choices that you make as a result of the information in this book or any advice or information you receive from me.

Please use this information responsibly.

Other Books by Joy Andreasen

Whispers of Joy, Outskirts Press, 2010, 978-1432760212

Whispers From Another Room, A Mystic's Journey Into the World of Spirit, Spirit Watch Enterprises, 2020 978-0989877121

Journey to Joy, A Psychic Medium's Story of Faith, Disillusionment, and Self-Discovery, Spirit Watch Enterprises, Second Edition 2021 978-0989877138

The Ancestor's Within: Discover and Connect With Your Ancient Origins, Brave Healer Productions, 2021(Joy wrote Chapter 3) 978-1954047358

TABLE OF CONTENTS

INTRODUCTION

The hardest part of writing this book was coming up with a title that hadn't been taken.

The number of books on sacred healing methods is astronomical! If you search of alternative healing methods, you will find everything under the sun, from allowing bees to sting you to covering yourself with leeches to consuming urine, and the list goes on and on.

I will be honest. I am not poking fun at these methods. I am just saying that I can't see myself doing any of these things. But I don't know what I may do if I was in severe pain or desperate for relief of some sort.

When I was a young adult, my ex-mother-in-law was from the mountains of West Virginia, and she swore by some of these methods. However, I never allowed her to pour pee in my ear for an earache.

When I was studying shamanism, I did participate in one sweat lodge. And that was enough for me.

I politely declined the class on walking on coals or putting them in my mouth. I decided I did not want to be buried in the ground for even a day. I never went alone out into the wilderness on a vision quest, although I am not completely eliminating the possibility of doing that one day.

The past day or two, I kept thinking about my mom who died of cancer in 2007. She was an Evangelical Christian whose faith kept her alive for years beyond the normal life expectancy of those with her type of cancer.

The word "miracles" kept popping up. It was my mom's favorite word.

I know. That word has a little bit of a nod to Christianity. My intention for this book is not to favor any belief system over any other.

A miracle is defined as "a surprising and welcome event that is not explicable by natural or scientific laws and is therefore considered to be the work of a divine agency." (Oxford Dictionary)

There are a multitude of people claiming to be "healers" who facilitate miracles using a variety of methods. But who is a healer and how do you know if you have run into a real one or even if you are a healer?

To me, a healing experience is when I have a session with someone and connect with my understanding of Divine Energy and bring that energy into this Earth experience so that it interacts with them in such a way that the experience creates a "miracle" for them. Something happens that cannot be explained by science but is a welcome and sometimes surprising change of events.

The person who facilitates this experience is thought to be a healer.

The first time someone told me I was a healer; I did not know what she was talking about.

When she told me, I was working at the Post Office. I wasn't a nurse or a doctor, and the sight of blood still makes me dizzy. Over the years, I have noticed that my tendency to faint upon entering a hospital has gone away, but a healer?

A healer is not just someone who works in the medical field. A healer is someone who assists others in achieving a sense of well-being. It has been suggested to me that in order to avoid being sued, I should choose a word other than "healer," since I have no certification or degrees in the medical field. I feel I have addressed those issues in my disclaimer at the end of the book.

We can all be healers if that means being kind, telling people they are wonderful, and wise, and amazing, especially if no one has ever told them that before. For that, we don't necessarily need a book to tell us how to do it. All we have to do is treat everyone with love and respect and every now and then do something nice or say something nice to someone.

But some of us seem to have a special ability to dig deep and get to the root cause of why people hurt and how to help them heal.

Healing is not a one-size-fits-all modality. We are all human. We all have lived as a soul for longer than just this lifetime. We are not just this particular body, this particular mind and this particular set of circumstances. We are complicated. We are born from complicated parents who were born from complicated parents. Our soul contains the remnants of memory of everything that has ever happened in this lifetime, all previous or alternative lifetimes, the time we spend in between lifetimes, the thoughts, emotions, beliefs and experiences of our ancestors, and sometimes even things that happen around us and to other people, known or unknown.

I have never really been a "follow the rules blindly" sort of person. When I began to explore various healing modalities, I found they only added to what I already felt inside or had already been doing.

Most of us who feel the "calling" to be a healer probably find this to be the case.

Over the course of my lifetime, I have studied a variety of spiritual paths and explored and studied a variety of energy healing methods.

As I developed new skills, I would want to teach them to others. I would have separate classes on various healing modalities such as Reiki and shamanic healing. I would find that sometimes during, for example, a Reiki class, I would feel compelled to throw in some shamanic healing technique or my guides would send me off on a "bunny trail" that had nothing to do with Reiki.

This is how I do what I call my "soul healing" sessions. I incorporate all of the skills I have developed or channeled from my guides over the years to lead the client on a path of healing soul, emotions, and mind which often results in a feeling of well-being physically as well.

Some of the techniques I have been given do not have a name or a title. There are no letters after my name giving me some sort of verified authority. I never went to college or received any degree of mastery other than my Reiki Master Teacher certificate. My guides don't give me a certificate of completion or mastery. Sometimes I will learn a skill, pay a significant amount of money for the skill, and then my guides will suggest that I am not to use that skill the way I learned it.

"NO. Don't do it that way - do it this way," they will say.

My shamanic teacher was aghast to find out that I had been performing soul retrievals for several years before "learning" how to do them. She was even more alarmed that I often performed them for people long distance and had the habit of putting their soul into a crystal and mailing the crystal to them. To be fair, I no longer do it that way, but at the time, it worked. She discouraged me from healing that way, but I continued to do them anyway. And people seemed to benefit.

So, what follows is my understanding and use of various healing modalities, with the disclaimer that they may or may not work for you! I never, *ever* diagnose illness, although I may "see" an energetic intrusion in someone's body and encourage them to get it checked out or work on it energetically.

Some of the skills I will mention merit their very own book, and in many cases, these books exist written by the people who discovered and perfected them. I will give credit to the source, with the statement that I may or may not use the healing tools exactly the way others use them.

We are all gifted with our own personal set of unseen helpers, a.k.a. guides, allies, power animals, angels, deities, healing team, or whatever you want to call them. Your guides are different from my guides. Your experience with these various healing tools will be different from mine. If you don't resonate with the word "guides" you can substitute that word for one that feels better to you. You may perceive that voice that speaks inside of you that is wiser and more evolved your "higher self" or "The Divine" or something else.

It is important to note that without my unseen helpers, I can't heal anyone or provide any valuable information or tools to bring about any sort of shift at all. I completely rely on my higher guidance to bring about healing or transformation of any kind. It is only through my relationship with what I normally just call "The Guides" that any of my clients feel any better at all. Some will say that I am accessing higher wisdom, what some people call "God" or that I am channeling my higher self or my soul. I will say, sure that is possible, I guess. However, when on occasion I ask for particular helpers, I can feel the energy shift. If a client resonates with a particular master like Jesus or Metatron or Mother Mary, I can feel their energy differently than when I just call "The Guides."

In this book, I may use the terms *The Divine, Divine Love, Creator of All That Is, Source Energy*, or possibly *God* or *Goddess* interchangeably. That energy that is formless and created the world of form has no gender, probably does not care what we call it, and is pure awareness, pure energy, and pure love. When I reference The Guides, I am not necessarily referring to The Divine, which is the energy that created the individual consciousness of The Guides. The Guides may be angels, beings from other planets or dimensions, ascended masters like Jesus or Buddha, or perhaps other life forms. I wanted to mention this distinction because I do feel it is important.

If you are reading this book, I am going to assume you have some interest in non-traditional healing modalities. This may be for personal growth and healing or you may have a desire to bring healing to others.

Reading this book in no way qualifies you as an expert or gives you the right to hang your shingle and call yourself a healer.

What *does?*

In indigenous tribes, healers do not call themselves healers. Shamans do not call themselves shamans. The title is given to them by their community and usually follows some sort of period of time when they are being taught or honing their skills. For me, I never really considered myself a healer. I called myself a spirit communicator. The spirits were the ones who were the healers and they told me what to do. Sometimes they would tell me to take this class or that class or they would tell me certain things I could not find in any book anywhere but it worked!

I believe and ascertain that healers are healers because of the results.

Does anyone benefit from what you are doing? Are people seeking you out because, "you helped so-and-so and maybe you can help me?" Are you using your skills on yourself and seeing results?

We don't just wake up one day and decide to be a healer. Well, maybe we do, but we don't immediately hang our shingle and go obtain a business license. We must have some sort of compulsion to be of service to others. We are allowed to make a living being a healer but we must not limit ourselves to a particular clientele or think we are going to get rich healing people. We must be people of character and care about the well-being of others and the planet and the fellow inhabitants of the planet, both living and dead. We must never use our skills to harm others or to bring about results that are not in the best interests of everyone concerned. And we cannot think that we know what the best always is.

I have been told by my guides to sometimes say no to a particular person or to refrain from offering healing energy or even what I call "positive energy" to someone. I don't know why. Sometimes their soul is not ready or sometimes they need to experience something that healing energy may interfere with. That is why it is so important to first develop a relationship with your unseen helpers before embarking upon any healing journey.

I spent many years practicing my skills on friends and family and those who found me before I ever labeled myself as a healer. For years I did not charge for my services, because I never obtained any sort of certification. I just knew what to do and I wanted to help.

Nowadays, I would say eighty percent of my clients are referrals from other clients. When you are skilled at what you do, word gets around. I don't really spend a great deal of time doing marketing. I tell The Divine that I am here to be of service, and I could use some clients, and somehow, they find me.

The Divine doesn't generally send you people who you can't help, unless you need to learn something from the experience. Source Energy seems to know your skill level and sends you people who can benefit from what you do.

Those of us who feel the pull to assist others to heal should be honing our skills continually and getting better at what we do over time.

None of us is so skilled that there is no room for improvement. We all get better and better as we go along. The more people we heal or align with a sense of well-being, the more we learn and get better at what we do.

It is all about creating a working relationship with your Unseen Helpers and creating an atmosphere where healing can take place. It is a co-creative relationship. The Guides can't do it without us and we can't do it without them.

Each of us contains a spark of The Divine within us. We live, we breathe, we are conscious creators whether we are aware we are doing it or not. We have abilities inherent inside of us. It is the understanding of that power that resides within us in combination with the power that is greater than us that creates change.

Some of us may shy away from specific words which denote this power. The words or labels we use do not negate the power that is inherent within any use of the power that is unseen to create change that we *can* see.

If you glean anything from this book, it is my hope that you discover the power that resides within you in partnership with the power that creates the miracles we all seek. We are The Divine in human form. We can create miracles in our own experience of life and we can assist others in shifting their experience of life as well.

HOW TO USE THIS BOOK

I recommend you read the chapters you feel drawn to and spend some time with one tool before you move on to the next. If you read this book from cover to cover and never incorporate any of it into your life or into bringing healing to yourself or others then, in my opinion, you have just wasted your time. Information without practical application is useless. I am one of those people who finds little use in knowledge that does not affect or change me in any way or at the very least make me a better person.

You may find that you resonate with some of what is detailed in these pages and not others. That is normal! Take the jewels and leave the rest behind. Not every healing technique is for everyone, or even works for everyone! I am a self-proclaimed self-help and spiritual book addict, and have at times only found one jewel in an entire book. However, that one jewel is worth the time and trouble of reading at least a portion of the book. If you are intuitive, you will be drawn to the tools that will become a part of your own "medicine bag."

I am not affiliated with any particular belief system but I am addicted to learning all about and honoring as many spiritual paths as possible. Some I feel a pull toward and some not so much. I refrain from passing judgment on any belief system or healing modality just because of what people or society have decided. I have a team of non-physical guides from various spiritual paths and they all seem to like each other! If a particular tool seems to be at odds with wherever you are spiritually, then by all means, set that one aside for now. If we are to be constantly evolving spiritually over the course of our lifetime, I would guarantee that one day that principle or tool may not seem so foreign to you at some point in the future. I would assume that perhaps one day some of the tools I am writing about now will no longer resonate with me. That is what growth is all about!

Be open to new ideas and new ways of doing things. Be open to perspectives other than your own.

If something doesn't feel good to you, set it aside.

Don't judge the path of others.

Bottom line. Use this book as you see fit, but please, *please, please*, **only** use these tools to bless, heal or benefit yourself and others. Never do anything that does not have the best interests of others and yourself at heart and never, *never*, try to interfere with the free will of another soul or their soul path.

Honor the principle: **HARM NONE**.

Feel free to change the way you use these tools as directed by your own team of non-physical helpers.

Have fun!

PART I

FOUNDATIONAL CONCEPTS AND EXERCISES TO ENHANCE YOUR SPIRITUAL PRACTICE

CHAPTER ONE

HEALING FOR BODY AND SOUL

"Health is the ideal balance between all major parts of our being (body, mind, and soul) in conjunction with our environment and everything we encounter."

Ted Andrews "The Healer's Manual"

What is healing, anyway?

The simple answer is that healing is the process of bringing yourself and others into alignment with your and their highest good: spirit, soul and body.

A healer is someone who assists others in the process of becoming aligned with a sense of well-being.

This is not the first healer's manual to ever be written and I am sure it won't be the last. Each of us has our own unique path and our own unique perspective based on our life experience, personality, and soul's mission.

We are not just the body we inhabit while in the earth plane. Our body is like our earth suit, giving us a means of experiencing life on this planet on which we live.

Although I have little recollection before the age of four or five, I noticed early on in life that I was not the person everyone perceived when they looked at me. I was the awareness that looked out from inside my eyes. No matter what was happening in my outside circumstances, I would notice my consciousness inside my body. I would notice my thoughts and emotions, and realize that the person inside was sort of stuck inside of a small child's body.

We are awareness.

What is the soul?

Is this awareness that looks out from inside our eyes what is commonly called the soul? Does that part of us even need to be healed?

Some will say the soul is that perfect, whole and complete aspect of ourselves, and has no need of being healed. It is our thoughts, emotions, and beliefs that are in need of healing. How do I separate the perfect, whole and complete parts of my soul from the shadows and the parts I try to hide? Can I separate myself from my shadow? Is my shadow separate from me, or a part of who I am?

Our soul is our life essence, and sometimes that part feels extreme emotions, experiences pain, ecstasy, terror and delight. Our life force may attach to those emotions, places and times where they occur, and get stuck there.

In various sects of shamanism and other belief systems, it is believed and taught that we actually have three souls. The way these three souls are described is a bit different depending on the belief system or the lineage of that belief.

Because I can't perceive of three separate souls living inside one body, I adapt that belief to an awareness of at least three aspects to the life force commonly thought of as a soul. The soul is that part of me that is eternal, has been with me since the beginning, has lived and breathed with me in every form I have ever taken, in every state of awareness, in every interaction with other life forms, in every moment of terror and joy and ecstasy, in my worst moments and my best, and loves me anyway.

What are these three aspects, and is that all there is?

In Shamanism it is taught that the first aspect is the part we bring in with us from other lifetimes. So, one aspect of your soul is the aspect of who you are or who you were in other states of awareness, other incarnations, even other lifetimes in other dimensions, other planets or star systems, and whatever happens in between incarnations. Most of us have lived lives as humans before, but even if we have not, most of us have lived lives *somewhere*, in some dimension. It is commonly believed that the soul is eternal. At some point our soul was connected to the God Source, whatever you want to call that. What happened before this moment in time is right there in the soul memory.

The second aspect to your soul is the part you inherit from those who share your blood. If you were raised by people other than your bloodline, then you carry part of their lineage as well! You carry within you the blood of your ancestors, their DNA, and with that you often inherit their joys, their challenges, their unresolved traumas, and, yes, sometimes their karma! Your tendency to lose your temper or the tendency to suffer from many illnesses can be traced back to your bloodline. In the Bible, Numbers 14:18 says the sins of the father can be visited upon the children to the third or fourth generation. We will talk about this more later, but the fact is, you don't only inherit your eye color, skin color, and hair color from your ancestors. You inherit patterns, beliefs, vows, cultural and ethnic tendencies and emotions, and so much more. Your DNA contains a blueprint for up to seven and some say as much as eleven generations.

The third aspect of your soul is the new part you create or experience in this incarnation. Some would argue that if you were in fact, raised by those who do not share your bloodline, this is the aspect of your soul which would include your experience with them. However, who is to say you don't share other lifetimes with those individuals? Who is to say that part of your DNA does not include them? But, bottom line, this third aspect of your soul is all new for this particular incarnation. This includes all of the joys and

21

fears, the beliefs, the traumas, the patterns, and of course the experiences that you as a soul living in a body have had while in this body during this time frame.

Other belief systems describe the three souls as the subconscious, the conscious, or the super-conscious. Or the lower world, the middle world, and the upper world. The part that is known, the part that is below us, or under the surface, and the part that is divine or above us.

 No matter whether you resonate with one of these theories of the three souls or not, your soul is not like a pie that is cut equally into three parts! If you are a young soul, you probably have a larger part that is inherited and experienced in this lifetime but a smaller portion from other lifetimes. If you have been around awhile, the portion of your soul that you bring in with you is probably running the show, with a smaller portion showing up from the other two aspects. Also, as you awaken and evolve in this lifetime and resolve certain pre-agreed upon issues, you may find that one aspect of your soul begins to take dominance over the others.

We are all aspects or living representations of The Divine, and have creative power to manifest amazing things on this planet and elsewhere. What about that?

Since The Divine is the energy or force that created all of the other experiences as a soul, I maintain that The Divine is inherent in all three aspects and possibly even more!

The paradox is that we are a living representation of Divine Energy and we are also separate and unique! We all bring with us a unique set of circumstances, life experiences, beliefs, traumas, thoughts and emotions, but we are also one with the life force of every living thing, and with all that ever has been and ever will be.

One of the mysteries of life is that *I am the All and the All is Me.*

Contemplating on the soul is akin to questioning the meaning of life and the mysteries of the universe!

It is important to consider what your understanding of the soul is before embarking upon a healing path. You don't have to agree with my suggestions of what a soul is and how it is important, but you do need some sort of base camp upon which to build your own structure of how to heal and why it is important.

What does the soul have to do with healing?

Everything!

Healing is not just eliminating illness from the body. Chances are, illness did not show up without a trigger, a circumstance that brought it on. Even those who are born with certain illnesses can usually trace that illness from somewhere. Grandma had it. A reaction to a vaccine brought this on. After so-and-so died, I never felt the same.

One of the first books I was introduced to when I began to shift my spiritual path from Charismatic Christianity to a more expansive and open-minded understanding of spirituality was a classic book by Louise Hay called *You Can Heal Your Life**. In this book, she outlines how our life experiences come as a result of our thinking. In it, she has a dictionary of common illnesses and their emotional and mental origins. When I first read the book, I did not immediately embrace all of her concepts, but I began to take notice of my own common maladies and do some internal inventory to see if I could relate to what she suggested as to the root causes. I found her observations to be eerily accurate!

Sometimes I get a cold because I have come into contact with germs, not because I am annoyed with someone, but I do find I rarely get a cold anymore! I used to be addicted to nasal spray for my constant congestion and apple cider vinegar for my frequent urinary tract infections, but these are almost non-existent these days! My doctor does not understand why, despite my MRIs, my back does not hurt. When I eliminated the source of my anger, annoyance, and financial worries, my illnesses seemed to disappear with it. Nowadays, it seems when I get knocked down physically, it is due to my tendency to overwork and rest too little. A couple of years ago my guides instructed me *not* to teach a master Reiki class and I decided to do it anyway (bad decision.) Right before the class, I came down with the worst bout of flu or something (tests had not yet been approved for Covid and I did test negative for flu) and had to cancel class for many months due to the onset of the pandemic. A coincidence? I doubt it. Would I have not gotten sick if I had listened to my Guides? I am not saying I was being punished for not listening, but as it turns out, I changed a lot of my techniques and learned some new things during the hiatus. Some of my students moved on, and I acquired new ones during that time.

We are not just the body we live in. Our body is just the part of our energy we see with our physical eyes.

Our energy body is comprised of four parts. We have our physical body, our mental body, our emotional body, and our spiritual body. We can get clogged up in any one of these bodies. Normally, an imbalance occurs somewhere other than our physical body first and if we don't address it, the imbalance eventually affects our physical body.

As we progress through the various energy healing modalities that I cover in the upcoming pages, we will address each of these bodies and various ways to correct the imbalances.

Suggested Reading:

The Healer's Manual – A Beginner's Guide to Energy Healing for Yourself and Others

Ted Andrews copyright 1993 and 2006 Llewellyn Publications

You Can Heal Your Life

Louise L Hay copyright 1984 and 1987 Hay House, Inc

Suggested Exercises for Chapter One

Take some time to contemplate the following questions. Journal about how you currently feel or what you believe to be true in relation to these questions.

Why do I want to heal?

What is my understanding of the soul?

How do I feel about this statement: *I am the All and the All is me.*

Do I want to heal myself or do I feel a pull to bring healing to others, or both?

I recommend spending some time in quiet meditation, journaling with these questions, and, if you feel drawn to the recommended reading, delve in!

CHAPTER TWO

THE POWER THAT CREATES CHANGE

One of the keys to effective energy healing and spirit communication is recognizing that we are not doing this alone. Yes, we have innate healing energy within us. We have wisdom and power within us. But where does that power come from?

The world of form is born through the world without form. Some call this God, the Universe, the Creator, the Source. This Source has no form but is inherent in everything we see, hear, taste, touch, smell, and sense. It is the creative force within us, and also the force of energy that has created the angels, guides, the ascended masters, the earth and other planet and star systems, the realm of nature and even what many call the dark side. Everything is born from this creative life force.

Yes, we are The Divine living inside a human vessel. There is within us a power that we do not continually access on a conscious level. However, if we think that we are healers without some sort of connection to a power source that is greater than the individual expression of our soul inside a single human vessel, we are fooling ourselves.

There are many spiritual paths which talk about the realization that The Power really resides within us. We don't need to go anywhere outside of ourselves to access that power. This is true, but in our human expression in a particular incarnation, we don't always recognize that we are actually divine. Yes, the power is within us, but the power is also outside of us. The Source is within every cell of every atom of everything that exists, yes also exists outside of all that is.

For me, I can connect with Source inside of myself. I can also connect with an understanding of a power source outside of myself.

Think of your soul like a cell phone. A cell phone has amazing capabilities. It can chat with people all over the world. It can give you news, games, social media postings, jokes, recipes, directions, and just about anything you can think of. It can suggest to you where to buy a new pair of shoes, and sometimes even know you are in need of a pair!

At some point, a cell phone needs to be hooked up to some sort of power source to regenerate its power. Depending on how much you are using it, it may have to be charged frequently or occasionally. Our soul is like that. We can run on our internal power source for a while. Depending on how much you are pulling energy out of your core, you may be able to go a little while, or a very long time in between charges; but eventually, you are going to have to hook yourself up to some sort of power source. You can go within yourself to that understanding that you are an aspect of that power, or you can go to your understanding of a power source outside of yourself. It makes no difference. If you are anything like me, I can tell when I have drained my power and need to hook up.

Religion and various belief systems exist in an attempt to hook us up to a power source. Some call the power source God, or Allah, or Jehovah, or Source, or my favorite, The Divine. That is all! The problem came when religious leaders became our power source instead of the power they were originally trying to represent. We began to depend on the leaders for our spiritual sustenance rather than going to The Source of Power for ourselves.

In my regular communication with various aspects of divine energy, I have found that The Source really is not attached to names, titles or affiliations.

27

I hear your protests now! *"What if I hook up with a power source that is dark or evil?"*

This is simple. If you plant a green bean plant, you are not going to grow a potato! In other words, if your intention is the highest good and healing for self and others, you are going to hook up to a power source that is compatible with your energy. In the same way all cell phones have to be charged by a cord that fits their unique design, you are only going to fit into the power source that fits with your energy.

The important thing is to rid yourself of any energetic debris that could be pulling you down to a lower expression of your soul or draining your internal battery. Anger, hatred, revenge, depression, grief, and fear are examples of lower-level frequencies. This is a process. We can't just choose not to be depressed anymore, or not to be worried or not to be afraid. We can choose to work towards aligning ourselves with the highest expression of our souls and ask to plug in to the highest vibrational power source available to us.

There are multitudes of ways to hook up to a power source and recharge your batteries.

In this chapter, I am going to suggest various ways for you to connect to the power source. I suggest you try them all and then decide which one feels best to you. You may also find that on occasion, your favorite one does not seem to be working and you may need to try something else. I am not sure why this happens, but it happens to me a lot. That is why I have various ways of connecting and charging up.

Meditation is a common suggestion to those who regularly engage in energy healing and spirit communication. And there are thousands of variations of meditation which I will not elaborate on here. I have several guided meditations on my YouTube channel, and besides me, there are thousands of other healers who have their own guided meditations.

Having experimented with a ton of different meditations, prayers, chants, shamanic journeys and various other power sources, I have found the breath to be a powerful tool for drawing into the body the energy of The Divine. It is probably my favorite. I sit quietly (or not. Sometimes I do this while sweeping the floor, while exercising, washing the dishes. Sitting quietly is not completely necessary). I focus on my breath. I visualize a cord of energy running down into the Earth Mother to hold me steady. I send another cord up to The Divine. I breathe. I pull the energy of The Divine into my body.

Connect. Breathe. Repeat. Done.

In the tradition of Shamanism, there are seven sources of power. There are the four directions of north, east, south, and west, and then there is above, below, and within. We have already chatted about the direction of within. Within must regularly be connected to the other power sources to remain a powerful source. The important thing to remember is that The Divine is inherent in the directions, the angels, guides, or whatever power source you choose.

In my meditations, I often combine the practice of focusing on the breath with calling in the directions and the power associated with the directions. I also add the archangels and Reiki symbols into the directions when I am calling them in. I have found this combination of practices to be most powerful in drawing in the presence of The Divine into the body. I offer the long version of my practice here. Feel free to alter it to fit your needs. I don't always do the long version. Sometimes I just imagine columns of light coming into my body from the six outside directions and connecting with the seventh direction, The Power Within. As I draw in my breath, I imagine The Power coming in through the columns of light into my body, and as I breathe out, I imagine The Power coursing throughout my energy body.

Here I offer my words of invitation to the powers of the directions.

Ho or Aho is a sacred Native American greeting. It is said before and after ceremony. Feel free to substitute for your own words if you feel led.

As you invite in the directions, draw in your breath and imagine the power and the archangel of that direction into your body. Breathe out and imagine the power coursing through your body. I face the direction I am calling in and either point with my hand, a crystal, or my intention, and draw a sacred circle as I face each direction. I often also light a candle. After the circle is complete, I face my alter and continue with the direction of above, below and within.

Ho, Sacred Power of the East, Brother Eagle, please come. Come bring illumination, the dawning of a new day, new beginnings, your wisdom and your insight into our ceremony today. Thank you for helping us to rise up just like the morning sun, ready to begin anew in our lives. We call upon the element of wind to blow into our lives those things that are ready to come to us, easily and without effort. I humbly invite Archangel Raphael, archangel of the east, of communication and healing to stand in the east in this circle. I call in all of my allies and spirit helpers, ancestral helping spirits and members of my spirit teams that hail from the east. Ho.

(You can say your own words. The theme is new beginnings, illumination, starting over.)

Ho, Sacred Power of the South, Sister Deer, please come. Come bring with you the warmth of the midday sun, helping us to manifest, to grow, to build upon what we have already started. Come with the gentle energy of the deer, bringing insight into our daily life. We call upon the element of fire to burn out anything that we no longer have need of, and to shine brightly to illuminate our highest path. I call in the energy of Archangel Michael, archangel of the south and of fire, please come. May you assist me/us as we shift energy, as we change and grow. May the change come powerfully yet gently as the deer so we are able to assimilate the change into our lives easily. I also call in my ancestral helping spirits, allies and other spirit helpers from the south. Please come. Thank you. Ho.

(Theme: manifesting, growing, sometimes changing what we are already doing, intuitive insight)

Ho, Sacred Power of the West, Grandmother Bear, please come. Help us to go within ourselves and find what we need to come out again refreshed. Give us the strength to let go of what needs to be released, to surrender our will to Divine Will. Thank you. We call upon the element of water, representing emotions and Spirit to help us use our emotions to connect with our highest plan and with Spirit. (You can call upon any deities that are connected with the element of water as well) I humbly request the presence of Archangel Gabriel, archangel of the west to come. As you brought news of the birth of Jesus to his mother Mary, you bring with you the energy of love, compassion, and releasing the old in anticipation of the new. Thank you for your loving and gentle presence. I also call in my allies, spirit helpers, and ancestral helping spirits from the west. Please come. Thank you. Ho.

(Theme: emotions, water, going within, surrender, the setting of the sun, endings)

Ho, Sacred Power of the North, brother Wolf, please come. Bring the wisdom of the ancestors, guides, and higher powers to help us to see things from a higher perspective. Thank you for all the answers the guides bring us. Thank you. We call upon the element of earth, the deepness of our roots, (ancestors, etc.) to help us grow and find wisdom. I humbly request the presence of Archangel Uriel, Archangel of Wisdom and Divination to come in and stand in the north, along with any other allies.

(theme: ancestors, guides, wisdom, element of earth)

You can also add:

Ho Great Spirit, (above us) thank you for coming to our ceremony. Thank you for the power of Spirit to shine on us and give us light. I call in the energy of Divine Love, Divine Light, Divine Healing Light, Divine Joy above us.

(theme: God, Higher Power, the power of the sun, Spirit of the Universe)

Ho Sacred Mother Earth, beneath our feet: thank you for coming. Thank you for giving us food to eat, water to drink, the life that we live comes from you. Thank you for all your blessings.

(theme: the Power beneath us, Mother Earth, all that She provides, the connection that we have with her)

Ho, Sacred Power that lives within us. I call in the wisdom of my soul, my higher self, my Holy Guardian Angel. Thank you for the wisdom that is within. May we be pure vessels that we might hear correctly and bring forth that which is within our own souls.

(theme: the power that lives within our own soul, inner wisdom, our connection to all that is)

I developed these words and rituals from my time with my shamanic mentor, Sue Wolfstar* as well as my studies into other belief systems and traditions.

I added in my own connection to specific archangels in the four directions which I received from my interest and research into High Magick* which includes specific angels into their rituals. Some add Metatron above us and Sandolphon beneath us. Sometimes I add Jophiel or my Holy Guardian Angel beside me. According to one tradition we are assigned an archangel depending on which day of the week we were born*. Mine happens to be Jophiel. I also add in the symbols of Reiki which you can do if you have been attuned to any of the sacred Reiki symbols.

In my exploration of various spiritual practices and viewpoints, I came across the practice of drawing in the breath to invite the energy of the Divine into the body as well as the particular angels of the directions. I found the combination of practices to be extremely powerful for me.

Most traditions begin calling in the directions in the east, since the sun rises in the east and is symbolic with new beginnings. At some point, my guides instructed me to begin in the north and end in the west. In this description, I began in the east to keep with tradition, however, feel free to start in whatever direction feels good to you. I understand many other traditions also begin in the north so I am not the only one. I recently was introduced to a form of Shamanism based out of Peru and they begin in the South.

Similar information can be found online. This is my own personal adaptation to the calling in of the directions. Over time I have personalized my opening up with the directions by calling in my main Guides who I have begun calling The Gatekeepers, and ask them to allow in the specific benevolent helpers that would like to work with me for a particular day or maybe a particular client. Different traditions attribute the directions with different elements and power animals. Feel free to adapt to fit your own traditions or affiliations.

In order to do readings or healings, you don't really have to do all this, but you do have to connect to a source that is greater and higher than you and your physical expression and awareness, or to be aware of your connection to whatever word you like to use to describe your understanding of *The Divine*. I do notice that the information that comes through is purer and more accurate and even specific when I specifically call in *The Creator of All That Is or The Divine* as well as The Guides and Angels and create a sacred circle of some kind. If you are doing a healing session, I do recommend you do some version of this. Remember: within your own limited understanding of human expression, you have no ability to heal. It is only through your teaming up with your higher guidance system that you are able to channel any healing energy and bring shifts to any individual or collective energy.

You will find that your ability to heal or to divine or to do almost any spiritual work is going to be influenced and dependent on your ability to understand and hold power in your body. The way that I have found to increase the power that I can hold in my body is to draw that power in through my breath and my intention.

If you are restrained by time or my way of calling in the Power seems too complicated, feel free to shorten this invocation by visualizing the seven directions all around you as streams of light and creating a light shield all around. You can simply say... I call in my allies from all directions and ask for your help and participation in this work.

Connecting with The Power does not have to be time consuming or complicated! It can be as simple as breathing! I cannot overstate the importance of making your spiritual practice a lifestyle! As I mentioned before, many times, throughout the day, I often find myself doing mundane tasks like washing dishes or sweeping the floor and I will turn to my breath and connect with The Power. There is an almost immediate connection! Remember that the Source Energy is all around us and inside of us and all we have to do is think about it and it immediately comes online. Unless my energy field is blocked or I am sick or tired, I feel energized and connected almost every time!

We cannot forget that we are The Divine living inside a human body. Our spiritual work, be it healing or manifesting a parking space is all about owning the Power that resides within us and accessing it to create change.

The Spiritualist community has a meditation called "Sitting in the Power." You can find guided meditations on YouTube helping you to learn this technique. It is not completely unlike what I have already described, but maybe a little less complicated. In this technique, you simply sit, place your awareness on your breath, and focus on the part inside of you that is divine.

My favorite thing to do is to connect with spirit while exercising! I love repetitive activity like the elliptical machine or walking. I used to run before a knee injury stopped that activity but any repetitive activity can act as a gateway to the spirit world.

In shamanism it is often a practice to use drumming or rattling to induce a trance-like state. This makes our brain waves slow down so we can receive intuitive information. It is impossible to connect with spirit when we are fully conscious and awake. We must slow our brain waves down to that daydream-like place where we often find ourselves right before falling asleep or doing other mindless activities. You can also use the ticking of a clock or the whir of a ceiling fan to get yourself to that state of awareness. Imagine your heart beat and your breath slowing down to the cadence of the tick of the clock or to other repetitive sounds. This is where spirit communication and connection occur!

You may also enjoy chanting as a means of quieting the mind and focusing your brain. There are tons of different chants.

My go to chant is OM MANI PADME HUM

What does it mean? *The jewel is in the lotus*. What does that even mean? To me, this is saying that only by going within ourselves can we find the treasure we seek. It is thought that repeating this mantra can lead to enlightenment. It seems to be the most popular and well-known chant in Buddhism. For me, it is the easiest one to remember so I do this one on occasion.

I like to listen to techno music and in my head repeat the chant to the beat of the music. I know this is not necessarily calming, but it does put me into an altered state of consciousness and often has the effect of creating a state of bliss inside my soul.

Back in my Pentecostal days, I used to spend hours praying in tongues. I would do it while I was cleaning, driving, cooking, running, or various other activities. Recently I was pleased to learn that the New Age community has their own version of praying in tongues that they call Light Language. It is the same thing! I told you, The Divine has no use for separation and labels. If you are familiar with Light Language or praying in tongues, it is a powerful tool for connecting with The Divine. For years I erroneously assumed that because I had said goodbye to Charismatic Christianity, I was no longer "allowed" to pray in tongues, but this is not the case! I did have to do some healing work on my soul based on my own individual wounds in regards to religious experiences, but after I had resolved my religious trauma, I do find that sometimes praying in tongues or engaging in Light Language is a beneficial practice.

Physical movement cannot be understated in this list of suggested activities for connecting with The Power. In Pentecostal circles we called it dancing in the spirit. Dancing and physical movement can often bring about a state of euphoria which aids in connecting with Spirit. This can be found in many spiritual traditions. In providing rituals for my clients to manifest certain things or even release certain things, I often add dancing to the ritual. I find it to be a powerful aid in bringing about a desired result. In healing, the desired result is an increase of power. The more power we can contain in our bodies, the more powerful healer we can become and the greater impact we will have on our own state of well-being as well as that of others. We all have seen indigenous tribes dancing for both celebration and ceremony. Physical movement is a powerful way to connect to The Power.

I restate this because it is extremely important.

Our ability to understand and hold power in our bodies is key to being a skilled healer.

The tradition of Reiki is the ability to draw healing energy into our bodies and channel this energy out of our hands into another person. If we cannot hold onto the power in our bodies, we are limited in our power to heal. Whether you use Reiki or some of the other healing techniques I will be sharing in this book, the ability to hold power inside of you and direct that power and awareness to an intended recipient is key to your success as a healer.

This takes dedication to spend time connecting with a Power Source and understanding your own power as the Divine living in human form.

Using the breath, we can draw into our bodies The Breath of Life and channel it like a missile to our intended destination. This is not to be taken lightly. We can effect change in our own lives and in the earth channeling the energy of The Divine and directing it to an intended target.

We always, *always, always*, do this with love and the intention of the highest good for everyone concerned. We always leave out our own desires, prejudices, judgments, and beliefs as much as possible.

Some believe and even teach that connecting to the Power can only be used for good and that the energy will never bring an undesired result. While it is true that the Power connected to the Source of All Life is complete and unconditional love and cannot do harm, this theory is based on the understanding of the Source as having opinions as to what is good and what is not. The Source Energy has no opinions or prejudices. It is not based on an affiliation of any kind. It is pure Source Energy. The truth is, if we connect with a power source when we are not in a high vibrational state and then channel that energy in ways that are in some way non-beneficial, there is the possibility that an undesired or non-beneficial result may occur. I always add an addendum to my work that says: for the highest good of all concerned.

That is why it is important to connect with our Power Source from a place of love and light and ask permission before sending energy to someone. It is also important to make sure you are connected to Unconditional Love.

There is a story in the Bible of Jesus cursing a fig tree and watching it wither before him. I never understood why he would have done this other than to show us that power can be used for good and for not so good.

Remember that when you use this power to benefit yourself in some way that may have an adverse effect on someone else, you are likely to regret doing so at some point. Even if you feel justified or feel that someone deserves it or whatever, remember that what you do does come back. In Wicca this is called the rule of three. Whatever you do, remember The Rule of Three. The energy you put out will come back to you three-fold.

The Power is neutral. The same nuclear power that can be a source of energy to power our lights and heat our homes can also be used to destroy and kill everything for miles around. Don't think that some force outside of yourself knows what you mean when you are directing this power. Be specific. Be kind. Use the power for the good of all concerned.

I was watching one of those fantasy shows on a streaming service the other day, and the witches in this show would draw their energy from one thing in order to empower something else. They would draw upon the energy of a flower to make a rock float and other such practices. Even though it is a television show, the principle here is that of: energy cannot be created or destroyed, it just changes form.

There are rituals you can do that affect others. Some of the effects are beneficial and some not so much. I am not saying it is never wise to do them. If I could stop a serial killer from murdering someone, I may consider it; however, I don't know everything. I don't know what the consequences are for interfering with free will in individual situations. For that reason, I tend to send the energy of Pink Light for the highest good for everyone involved in any given situation. Pink is the color of compassion and Higher Love and to direct it to someone with no thought of what it is to do specifically will have the effect of enhancing their own understanding of the light of their soul and align them with their highest good. I tend to remove myself from a desired outcome when doing this ritual.

Once I had an individual who was in the practice of continually maligning me. This had been going on for years, and I was aware. I had created an energy shield which worked most of the time. At some point, I became aware of a ritual using a piece of red velvet cloth cut out in the shape of a tongue which would create the experience of him becoming tongue-tied every time he attempted to malign me. The only reason I decided not to do it is because I knew that this ritual would affect me as well, and I was not sure in what way it would affect me. I also knew that this ritual would keep me energetically tied to him. I eventually decided to give this person no thought or energy whatsoever in my mind. I did not bless him or curse him. I never mentioned his name and when in conversation his name would come up, I would attempt to change the subject or leave the conversation.

Remember. What we think about grows. Energy follows thought. Focusing on what you don't want often has the opposite result than the one you desire. If you use energy or power to change something you don't want, you may experience the opposite result from your desire.

When we channel the energy of the Divine and use it for something, it is vitally important for there to be an exchange of energy. When I ask my Guides for something, I say thank you. I often present them with gifts by giving fruit, coins, or other items to them as a gift. I give gifts of charity. I am kind to others. I leave extra money in parking meters for the next person. I send out healing energy into the air and ask that whoever needs it may have it, knowing that I will never know where it went and I will never receive any credit for it.

39

I also often engage in the practice of gratitude. I thank my pillow for being so soft under my head when I am sleeping. I thank my plants for giving me beauty and purifying the air I breathe. I thank my spiritual tools for their service to me. When I am out walking, I mentally send blessings to every tree, flower, bird, or fellow traveler on the walking path coming and going.

In doing this I am establishing and maintaining a connection to the consciousness in all the other conscious expressions of form around me. When I do this, I find that I seem to get feedback and assistance even when I don't necessarily ask for it.

I find that when I ask for something that I am not ready to handle or is not in my best interests, there seems to be walls that the energy of my requests bounces off of. If I try to go somewhere or do something that is not in the higher plan, my attempts are met with frustration and failure.

If you find that your attempts to connect with power are met with frustration, try a different approach. Take a break. This path may not be for you at this time. Go easy on yourself. Connecting with Spirit should not be hard or take a lot of effort on your part. It should be joyful and bring you much satisfaction.

I have tried to offer you a variety of ways to connect to your Power Source. This is because we are all unique and what works for me may not work for you.

Connecting to a source of Power and understanding yourself as an expression of that power in human form is essential to being a good healer. Without it you will experience limited results or none at all. This step cannot be skipped.

Before we move on, let's take a moment to discuss our right to connect with the power of The Divine and our understanding that we are a living representation of that power.

Many times, we feel unworthy to stand in our power and command change to take place. We are making requests of the Benevolent

Helpers with a belief that they are stronger or higher or wiser or more powerful than we are. We are requesting them to do the work rather than realizing that we are co-creating with them.

When my dad was alive, he was a master at changing the weather. He lived in Florida for over thirty years and successfully changed the course of a number of hurricanes so that it either missed the area where he lived or best-case scenario, went out to sea. I never heard him once say, "Oh God if it be Your Will, please make this hurricane shift courses." Yes, he was accessing the power of the Divine through his own belief system, which happened to be Charismatic Christianity, but he would stand in the Power and command those storms to move or change course.

Once he came to Virginia to visit and the weather forecast was dismal. He stood up and said, "NO! I command the rain to cease in the name of Jesus!" He stood on the fact that if Jesus could calm a storm, then so could he. Within the hour, the downpours stopped and it did not rain for the rest of his visit.

After returning home, the weather continued to be sunny for a couple of weeks. Finally, I called him and asked him to rescind his request so we could have some rain! A half hour later, it rained.

When I decided to go exploring other spiritual paths, I was hesitant to *command* anything to happen! I would make requests, and even offer gifts to the spirits in charge, and that worked for me, most of the time. I kind of forgot about authority and how well it had worked for him.

Recently, dad showed up from the other side and reminded me that we do not have to shy away from our authority to facilitate change. We *can* command our blessings and changes to occur. If we don't believe in our own authority, how are the spirits to believe us? Yes, it is important to keep in mind the highest good for everyone concerned, but it is okay to command change and expect that change to happen.

Having an understanding of authority and the right to command change is inherent in our relationship with our guides, our understanding of our power and the power of The Divine to create change, and our belief that this is possible.

Now, I will add the addendum that some things you can command all you want and change will not occur. My mother still died of cancer despite my dad's prayers and commands to the contrary. At the end of his life, when he was well into his eighties, he slipped and fell in the kitchen, hitting his head and causing internal bleeding in the brain. He became unable to communicate and slipped in and out of consciousness. I became extremely agitated when his pastor came to his bedside and commanded him to rise and be healed. I thought that probably dad should be the one to decide whether he wanted to wake up or go on to the other side, and after the pastor left, I told him so. He passed a couple of weeks later.

How do we determine what we can command to change and when to not waste our time?

Sometimes we just know.

I just knew that the pastor was wasting his time commanding my eighty-five-year-old dad to rise up and be healed. We cannot know what is right for someone else.

Sometimes our soul has contracted before birth to experience certain things. In those times, we can command all we want and nothing will happen.

Sometimes we need to get to the root of why something is happening. In the upcoming chapters, we will learn a variety of methods of releasing emotions, beliefs, and other obstacles that keep us from healing.

I believe that the reason there are a number of different tools to facilitate a similar result is because there are times when one tool does not work, but another one will.

Why?

Who knows. That may be a question for another day.

Suggested Exercises for Chapter Two

Try the various ways of connecting to the power of the Divine. See if you can *feel* it in your body. Try them all before deciding which ones work best for you.

Journal about your understanding of the Power and your thoughts or hesitation about channeling that power and holding it in your body.

Choose a situation in your life that you would like to change. Think about whether the changing of this will affect others in a non-beneficial way. If not, come up with a statement and command the situation to change.

You can say, "I command my highest good in the area of ......"

You can try this on easy things first before choosing something difficult. I like to command green lights and short lines at the store. I don't command parking spaces unless it is raining or cold because I am sure my highest good is to walk. I also command the energy of love and joy in my home and work space.

Be creative! Command family get-togethers to be pleasant and drama-free. Command that you will easily find what you need at the grocery store.

On a larger scale, command abundance or health or well-being in accordance will the highest good for everyone concerned. Don't command something that will hurt someone else. Command that what you want will come to you in a way that is easy and beneficial.

If you don't know what the highest good is, you can direct Pink Light toward a situation for the highest good of everyone concerned.

*Susan Wolfstar, Shamanic Healer and Medical Intuitive

https://www.wolfsongsschool.com

*Angel Healing & Alchemy – How to Begin, Angela McGerr copyright 2015 Axix Mundi Books

 ISBN 9781782797425

*High Magick Damien Echols copyright 2018 Damien Echols and Sounds True ISBN: 9781683641353

CHAPTER THREE

DEVELOPING YOUR INTUITIVE MUSCLES

In traditional medicine, having intuition is not really a requirement; although, there is no doubt it would be beneficial. Rather than running a battery of tests, wouldn't it be nice to know that pain in Mrs. Smith's chest is not heart related, but because she has a pulled muscle or indigestion?

However, in energy healing, connecting to your psychic senses is vital to being able to transmit healing energy.

In systems such as Reiki, you don't really have to be all that intuitive in the basic practice of transmitting the energy of healing to another person. In reality, you don't really have to feel anything. You trust that the energy is coming into your body and flowing out through your hands. Whether you are in the presence of the person or if you are sending it long distance, all you really need is faith in your connection to the Source.

However, doubt is like a kink in a water hose.

If you don't have faith that you are a skilled conduit for the healing energy to flow, you will probably have limited results.

When I was first introduced to Reiki, a popular healing modality which originated in Japan and has gained popularity all over the world over the past hundred years or so, a friend of mine explained to me what this healing modality was and gave me my first Reiki experience. In Reiki, the teacher transmits the ability to heal into your energy field by what is commonly called an attunement. Initially, I felt absolutely nothing. My hands didn't tingle or get hot, like so many who have had the experience. Since I was studying Shamanism at the time, I put Reiki on the back burner and did not really think much about it for another year or so. The woman who gave me my first attunement to Reiki said that I was already attuned, that the attunement she gave me was just a formality, and that is why I didn't feel any different. However, on occasion I will have students who report the same experience. My thoughts were that I was not really focused on the experience and did not completely understand it, so my experience was limited. Remember, what you focus on grows!

If you are doing your daily meditation or spiritual practice, you will probably begin to notice that you are receiving some intuitive hits. Connecting and developing with your source of power and developing your psychic muscles goes hand in hand!

In the next chapter, I will cover connecting with your Guides and learning to channel their energy into your body. In order to do that you have to be confident that you are receiving evidential information. The Guides can't come in if you don't believe that you are actually experiencing anything.

So many people say they can't visualize or receive information, but this is not true. The following exercise will prove this to you.

Exercise: Understanding the Psychic Senses

Close your eyes. Take a few calming, cleansing breaths. Breathe in. Count to 4. Breathe out. Count to 4. Do this a few times and allow your thoughts to focus on counting and your body to relax. Feel your muscles relax and your brain waves begin to slow down.

When you feel calm, imagine with your eyes closed a pizza sitting on a table in front of you. See the pizza. What kind of crust is in on the pizza? What kind of toppings? Notice what the pizza smells like. Take a breath and imagine the scent of the pizza. Imagine you are sitting at the place where you normally eat pizza. What sounds do you hear? Listen to the conversation around you. Who is there with you? Are you in a restaurant or at home? Now, imagine picking up a piece of pizza and holding it in your hands. What does it feel like? Do you feel the warmth of the pizza? Do you feel the grease running down your hands? What emotions are coming up for you? If you like pizza, how do you feel? If you don't, what is your reaction? Now, take a bite of the pizza. What does it taste like? What toppings did you taste? What is your mind telling you about the pizza? That it is wonderful? That it is bad for you? That you are going to have a reaction in your body? Do you have a memory of something that happened before when you ate pizza that is affecting your experience of it now? Do you have a judgment about what pizza does to your body?

When you have experienced everything that is related to having a bite of the pizza and feeling it in your mouth and noticing your thoughts and emotions and judgments about the pizza, you can finish this exercise and open your eyes.

If you were successful at seeing, feeling, tasting, smelling, and knowing what you know about pizza, you can develop your psychic senses! You were using all of them!

A wise shaman once said to me, "Spirit is everything that happens when your eyes are closed."

If you have reached this stage in your journey, you understand that every natural sense: sight, sound, taste, touch, and smell have a psychic counterpart. Then you add knowing, feeling and remembering and you have it covered!

47

You will be using all of these senses when doing healings or spirit communication, so you need to familiarize yourself with each one and trust what comes through.

The biggest hurdle you will have when developing your psychic senses is not believing in yourself and your ability to receive information.

So how do you develop your psychic senses?

This will take some time and practice, but your Guides are your personal trainers in psychic development!

So, which comes first, connecting with your Guides or developing your psychic senses? I am not sure you can do one without the other, but here are some exercises to get you started. These exercises develop the ability to focus and to attach meaning to things you "see", so I am going to include them here.

Exercise 1: Notice What You Notice

Close your eyes and take a few moments to focus on your breath. Count to 4 while breathing in. Count to 4 while breathing out. Notice your body relaxing. Notice your thoughts quieting and your heart rate slowing.

With your eyes closed, begin to focus on the objects in the room where you are sitting. Go around the room and notice details. Begin to focus on the feel of the fabric of specific items, their color, and how they make you feel. Notice any sounds you hear.

Allow your imagination to wander a bit. Imagine you have a magnifying glass and can get into the corners, under the floor, above the ceiling, beyond the walls. What is under the rug or inside the closet?

Use as many of your psychic senses as possible.

Now focus on a specific object in the room or even one that may or may not be there, like a spider on the wall. (It can't hurt you, it is not physically there, silly!) Hone in on that spider. Get closer to it. Put aside your fear of spiders for a moment. See it really, really close. What is it doing? If it could talk, what would it be telling you? Imagine you could feel what the spider is feeling. Imagine you could communicate with it. If you get really, really close, what happens next? This is important! Don't recoil, surrender to the experience. Allow yourself to imagine what happens next and what the spider does, what you do, what you say, what the spider says, how the spider feels, what is happening in its body, even what the spider is thinking about. Does the spider feel male or female? Young or old? Friendly or aggressive or afraid?

When you are finished, open your journal (I assume you have one. If not, get one!) and write the message you received. You may not know what it is until you begin to write.

This is how it works.

While I was writing the exercise, I was doing it inside my head. I noticed the spider on the wall. No, not a physical spider. A "spirit" spider. I got closer. I felt her energy. She was female. She was old. Her name was Grandmother Spider. I even saw the hairs on her legs and felt her stiffness inside of her legs. She told me she was helping me to write this book because I was weaving various healing modalities into a web of connection that would help others to heal. She also told me it was about time for me to take a break and go exercise because my legs were getting stiff. (Yes, I sometimes get lost in time when I am writing.)

You see how that works? Everything I "saw," "heard," or "felt" was significant, right down to the stiffness I felt in Grandmother Spider's legs. I received a message from my soul and from the

49

spirit of Grandmother Spider. I surrendered to the experience and allowed it to unfold.

Eventually, you will be able to use this method to tune into the energy of yourself and others and "see" information that will guide you to heal. If you see the spider's heart, you will focus on the heart. (I assume spiders have hearts, I don't even know, and it doesn't even matter.) If you are drawn to her legs, you will focus on the legs, etc.

If you do this exercise repeatedly, eventually you will begin to allow it to take you to where you need to go to receive information about yourself and others. One day you may see a door where there is no door. You may walk through it in the exercise and see something or someone on the other side of the door you need to see. You may open a closet door and see a skeleton, letting you know you perhaps need to "come out of the closet" or that there is a secret of some kind that needs exposing and releasing. You may see a dust ball on the floor, indicating there is some sort of cleaning that needs to be done.

Remember that everything you notice in this exercise is symbolic and the fact that you noticed it means it has a message for you.

Exercise 2: Focus and Receive a Message

With your eyes closed, imagine a common item you see frequently. It could be a red ball, a toy train, your cat, or whatever comes to mind. Try to hold that item in your mind's eye for as long as you can. Look for details on that item, such as the variations in color, sound, smell, taste, or touch. Imagine how that item makes you feel. If that item had a message for you, what would it be?

This is similar to the exercise where I saw a spider on the wall in my room and received a message from her.

You are going to need this skill when doing healings or receiving information for your intended recipients!

It may be a good exercise to set a timer, meditate on a red ball or single item, and see how long you can do so before your mind wanders. Look at the timer and notice how long you were able to hold the image of the red ball. Each time you do the exercise, set the timer and try to hold the image longer.

Instead of focusing on an image of a red ball, you can try counting backwards from 100 to 1, breathing in to a count of four and out to a count of four, focusing on a feeling like Divine Love, Peace or Joy, finding an object in your field of vision and holding that vision as long as you can, or holding the vision of a favorite deity or angel or master. Anything you can do to hold your focus as long as you can, is an exercise that will take you far in being able to hold a link from Spirit.

When you are doing energy work, essentially you are creating a cord of energy or a link from your awareness to a Higher Power. After you have created this link and practiced holding it for a length of time, you will be drawing in the energy from the Higher Power and channeling it to your intended recipient. I like to think of it as a triangle. You are creating a cord or a link to the Higher Power, and then you are intending a link to be created from that Higher Power to your intended recipient. You can channel the energy down into your body and out through your hands, your third eye or your voice, or you can create a link down from the Source directly into your recipient through the top of the head, or the crown chakra. This requires the ability to hold your focus in a singular and concentrated way for an extended period of time. This is why these exercises are important.

Suggested Exercises for Chapter Three

Do the previously suggested exercises and journal about the information received.

Meditate on the information in this chapter. Journal about how you feel about the information. Think about how this information is enhancing your spiritual practice and lifestyle.

CHAPTER FOUR
CONNECTING WITH GUIDES

Not everyone who uses psychic ability consciously connects with guides or source energy. As I mentioned in the last chapter, doing energy work consists of creating a cord of energy between you, your source, and your recipient. Many who do psychic readings simply create a cord or a link between them and their recipient without connecting to source energy.

In order to connect with another person or animal, you have to create an energetic link between you and them. The same is true for connecting with a guide. When connecting with a guide for another person, you must create an energetic triangle. The guide is at the top of the triangle, with you and the other person at the other two points and the lines of the triangle are energetic links that connect the three of you.

To connect with another person psychically, all you need is the link between you and them. Essentially, you are connecting to them and then "reading" what you see in their aura.

And to connect with a guide, all you need is the link between you and the guide.

The reason why it is sometimes hard to connect is because your energy is not in sync. The other person may have created a block or perhaps you did. It is also a little like tuning in to a radio frequency. You have to tune in your dial properly to get good reception.

If you are connecting with Source Energy, you may not consciously be connecting with guides, but I find it helpful. I also find it easier to just say, "The Guides" rather than referring to The Source and then the Guides, but I have found it extremely beneficial to go to The Source first and then access The Guides.

You may have one healing guide or you may have a team of them. Don't limit yourself to just one!

I have a team of seven that I call my healing team. I invite them into my sessions with clients when I am doing my calling in the directions, as described previously. When I call them in, I normally call them in from the direction of east, since most of them seem to originate there, but one of them comes in from the south and one from the west. Sometimes I sense their presence individually, but most of the time it is more of a collective energy. They don't come in every time. Normally the ones who need to be in the room for whatever my agenda is for that day will show up. Sometimes I will "feel" which ones show up since they each have an individual essence.

Do you choose your guides or do they choose you?

For the most part, they choose you. Sometimes you can call upon someone specific if you happen to know of a specialty they may have or that your client identifies with some specific belief system or master.

I was once invited to a person's house who had breast cancer to do Reiki. Immediately upon entering her home I felt a presence that was blue in color. I described what I felt and she let me know that she prayed to Shiva. He is blue. I had previously not been in his presence nor been introduced to him, but I felt him upon entering her house and he assisted me in the healing session.

Recently I connected to a client's guides and they seemed to be fighting with one another! She confirmed that, yes, she found they often did not agree with each other when she tuned in to them. I suggested that she go up to The Divine first and access her guides from a higher perspective.

Is this even possible? Do guides disagree with one another?

Obviously, yes.

I once bought a Mayan god from a local vendor in Mexico. When I brought it home, it did not get along with my other spirit helpers. I woke up in the middle of the night and it felt like a thunderstorm in the house. I ended up having to separate the Mayan god from all the rest. I imagine the god eventually went back home although I still have the statue in my family room. I haven't felt anything from it recently. If a god is not compatible with you or your other spirit helpers, they will eventually work it out. If not, you have to work it out for them and let them know they have to get along.

There are spirits that are conscious and aware that are connected with local deities. A lot of these are earth-based spirits and so are living in earth-based frequencies and levels of awareness. I am not opposed to having these as your spirit helpers as long as they understand that you intend the highest good for yourself and for your intentions. If you go to the Divine first and ask that the highest and best spirit helpers be assigned to you and that the ones you end up with work from the highest available frequencies, you should be okay.

Remember that you receive spirit helpers that are compatible with your frequency. If you want some really highly evolved guides that don't fight with each other and emit a higher vibration, you have to consistently keep your vibration high. You have to live in peace and love and joy to the best of your ability and desire to serve others and be a positive force of love and joy wherever you are. If your life is filled with drama and you find yourself constantly at odds with others or sick or depressed, you will not be able to connect with a highly evolved spirit helper.

Are spirit helpers and guides the same thing?

I believe we have multiple guides and spirit helpers, and I use these terms interchangably. When we experience an awakening of sorts or a shift in our vibration, sometimes our guides will switch out or become more active or inactive. If they cannot connect with us due to an incompatible vibration, they can't really help much.

How do I connect with my guides?

All you need to connect with your guide or guides is the desire to do so. You really don't need specific information about them or even really to feel their presence right away. Initially, all you need is a desire to connect and the faith that you have, however, over time you may get to know them and feel their presence when they enter the room.

Connecting with guides is as easy as imagining a column of light from the top of your head traveling upwards to where they are.

It is important to get yourself into a bit of an altered state of consciousness, kind of like you are daydreaming, as we discussed earlier.

Here is an exercise to connect with a guide or group of guides.

Exercise: Connecting With Your Guides

Sit in a comfortable place, or do what you do to connect with Spirit. (As I mentioned previously, you don't have to be sitting still or in a specific position.)

Breathe in to a count of 4. Breathe out to a count of 4. As you focus on your breath, notice your heartbeat and imagine it is slowing to a relaxed pace. Notice your body relax. Continue to breathe in and out and focus on the feeling of love and joy. This raises your frequency so you can make contact.

If you are sad, depressed, sick or angry you may have a difficult time connecting with your guides. It is important to travel up the emotional frequency wave to a higher frequency so you will have an easier time being an energetic match to their vibration. Love, joy and peace are the highest frequencies.

When you feel your frequency shift to a high vibration, say, "I now wish to connect to my guide."

Just as described previously, just notice what you notice. You may see a color, feel an emotion, hear a sound. You may actually see their presence, or you may not. You may see an angel, an ascended master, an animal, a deceased loved one or pet or any number of other possibilities. The initial contact depends on your faith in your ability to connect and your trust in your own intuitive hunches.

Spend some time with them! You can ask questions, you can just sit in their presence, whatever feels good to you. Afterwards, you may want to journal about your experiences.

If you don't see or hear anything, don't doubt the experience. Sometimes it takes time to build up the ability to hold the frequency so they can come through. Keep doing your spiritual practice regularly and one day they will show up!

If you feel connected to a specific master such as Jesus, Buddha, or Mother Mary, it is okay to ask if they will be your Guide. After I left traditional Christianity, I was not interested in connecting with Jesus at first. He would show up on occasion, but it took awhile for me to reestablish my relationship with him. If you have been wounded by religion or religious people, you may not want a relationship with some religious figures. They are okay with that! This was an important aspect of my path, because if Jesus and I had remained good friends, I may have not felt the need to go exploring other paths, and based on a dream I had when he was encouraging me to go off the traditional path, I know this was the plan all along. Now he shows up pretty frequently and is part of my healing team!

If you do end up with a team, they may introduce themselves together as a group or individually. My team introduced themselves individually and I would ask them if they wanted to be part of my team.

If a guide connects with you or joins your team, does this mean they will be a part of your team forever or do they sometimes come and go?

This may seem like I am repeating myself, but this is worth a little further exploration.

I find that the guides have specialties. If I am in need of a plumber, I am not going to call a doctor. I may know their specialties and call on the ones that are most suited to the needs at hand, or I may just tell them what I need and have faith that the right ones will show up. Most of the time, I don't overthink it. When I open up my altar in the morning and call in the directions, I tell them my agenda and ask that the right ones will show up for the clients that are scheduled that day or for the needs at hand. And then I let it go.

When a client shows up, or calls or whatever, I will create a link to the guides and another link to the client and off we go.

Sometimes your guides will just show up for you in meditation. This happened to me a lot in the beginning. Because I was mostly unfamiliar with gods and goddesses, I had to look up who they were after I came out of the meditation.

I also found that sometimes people are not open to various deities so be careful who you share with. I once lost half of my students after sharing that a particular deity showed up for me in a meditation. It ended up it was more of a message of things to come rather than a god becoming part of my team. Don't assume that particular gods and goddesses are good or evil. Sometimes they come in to share a message or warn of things to come. It does not mean they are energetically compatible with the rest of your team. If you are vibrating at a high frequency, you will not be appealing to lower-level energies.

Can animals be guides?

Yes! These are commonly known as animal allies, power animals, totem animals, etc. I have found that I have a couple of regular power animals that seem to be around most of the time and then I have some that come and go depending on what I happen to need. Only one of them is part of my healing team but the rest come and go as they are needed.

You can connect with them the same way or through a shamanic journey, which I will describe later.

Let me stress here that it is really not necessary to get specific information about who your guides are, how many you have, or what their names are. Most of them are not all that interested in that, only that they are there to assist you. A lot of the time I am not asking specific guides to come in. I connect with the feeling of love and joy, usually through sending my awareness out the top of my head to the highest frequency I can connect to. When I feel a sense of joy, I know I am connected. I am assuming they know who is needed and are all connected to each other and me.

Suggested Exercises for Chapter Four

Continue to do your exercises from previous chapters.

Do the suggested meditation to connect with at least one guide.

Notice how it feels to be in the presence of your guide.

Write down any of your impressions.

CHAPTER FIVE

OUR ENERGY BODY AND CHAKRAS

I am assuming if you are reading this book, you have some understanding of some of the basic principles of energy and our energy bodies, but since I really don't have any way to know exactly where everyone is on their healing journey, I am going to cover a few basic principles here. If you are already familiar, feel free to skip ahead. I just want to make sure all of the bases are covered before we get into the work of healing.

If your understanding of these principles is different from mine, feel free to adapt to fit your own perceptions and knowledge.

Even if you are familiar with these principles, you may want to refresh your memory and see if I may have some perspective that you can add to your own understanding. I also include some exercises at the end which you may find useful.

I mentioned before that we actually have four bodies. Here is a description of each energy body and what kinds of blocks and intrusions commonly occur in each one.

Spiritual Body

The outermost layer of our energy field is our spiritual body. All of the other layers of our energy body are encased inside of this layer. This is the part of us that is spirit. Because it is the layer that surrounds the other layers and can extend several feet around our physical body, it is no surprise that this layer often is the one that touches other people and animals and life first before we sometimes are even aware. It is also the part of us that is directly connected to the energy of life and the Divine Presence. It is the part of us that has spiritual experiences, that connects to our sense of the Divine. We can be very connected to this part of ourselves or very disconnected. It can extend many feet from our physical body or be very close. Our energy bodies are fluid. Sometimes they are open, light, and airy, and sometimes they are very thin and heavy. When we are faced with something that we don't trust or feels off, it is likely this part of us that felt it first. When we get wounded by a religious body or a concept of the Divine, this is the part that was probably affected first. People who sense non-physical energy like ghosts or angels most likely have a very active spiritual body. Sometimes it is important to shield this part of us when we become too overwhelmed or when we find ourselves bothered by spirits.

Emotional Body

Our emotional body is the next layer in from our spiritual body. We all know what emotions are. They are the good, the bad, and the ugly that rest here inside of our spiritual body but right next to our mental body. Most likely, you experience an emotion first before you develop a belief or a mental pattern. For example, if you have a belief that "I am not safe" which would probably be located in your mental body, you most likely experienced an emotion of fear first. Normally you would need to experience an emotion over and over before you develop a belief which then gets lodged in your mental body. Emotions and beliefs go hand in hand.

Mental Body

Right inside the emotional body and next to the physical body is the mental body. This is where thought happens. We normally have to have a thought multiple times before a belief is formed. Emotions, thoughts, and beliefs can originate in any of our energy bodies and get lodged there, but if unaddressed, will eventually make its way to the physical body.

Physical Body

This is the part of us that we can see, feel, and touch. It is not just our organs, bones, muscles and blood. It is the physical expression of all of our other bodies!

These four energy bodies are not four distinct and separate parts of us. They don't layer us like we may wear layers of clothes in the wintertime. They are fluid and changeable, constantly interacting with one another and radiating out of one another. It is kind of like seeing steam coming up from the road in the summer. Depending on what activity we are engaged in, one of our energy bodies may be more active or more dormant.

As a healer, you will find that you can sense a person's energy body if you try. Start by holding your hand several feet away from another person and slowly move closer and closer to their physical body. You will feel the energy closer to their body become more dense, perhaps warmer, perhaps colder, depending on their health or state of mind. You may find the energy shifts very close to their body or further out in different areas of their body. This is using your sense of touch but also your intuitive sense of touch. Some people can see auras, which is another name for the energy body. The aura may radiate in various colors, depending on the person's general vibration or how they are feeling or what they are doing at the moment. Even if you don't physically see auras, you can train yourself to intuitively see colors around a person. This can assist you in sensing a person's general state of mind or even whether they are someone you may like or need to stay away from.

The ability to scan a person's energy field and sense their general state of health and what areas you may need to focus on is a vital skill to being a good healer. You will need to develop your intuitive muscles in order to be able to receive this information. Often when I am doing a healing, I will feel pain in an area I need to address in the client. This is also true for spirit communication, but we are not specifically learning that skill here. It is important before you engage in a healing session that you are aware of your own state of health and any areas of discomfort so you don't mistake those pains for the pains of your client, or vice versa. If you feel an area of discomfort in your own body when you are scanning another person's energy field that was not there before, there is a good chance the pain is not yours. Depending on your own intuitive strengths, you will need to access information about your client in a way that works for you. You may see areas of congestion in a person's energy field as cloudiness or dark spots. You may see actual organs if you are educated in anatomy. You may hear sounds. You may see images that remind you of certain things. You will need to practice so you can trust your intuitive hits. Don't worry if the person doesn't acknowledge what you are intuitively picking up. Sometimes imbalances occur in the energy field before they show up in the physical body. Never doubt your intuition, regardless of the reaction of your recipient.

Your own self confidence is your most important tool in your medicine bag! This comes from building a relationship with your Healing Guides and practicing developing your intuition.

Once I was tuning in for a client and giving her a message from her grandmother, who showed me her dishes. The client confirmed that yes, she indeed inherited her grandmother's dishes. Then her grandmother showed me one of the plates, and on it was raw meat. I recognized the meat as liver, because it has a different texture than any other meat before it is cooked. This may seem like a strange message, but as it turns out, the client's brother is struggling with liver disease which came from the inherited tendency toward alcoholism. The client confirmed that her grandmother would have something to say about her brother and his struggles.

It took me a moment to interpret the message for the client, but using my intuitive sight, I saw the liver on a plate, and was able to ascertain that the liver disease was based on an inherited tendency. I also shared a common shamanic belief that if eating a specific meat from an animal may have a healing effect on the corresponding body part. So, I suggested maybe her brother may include liver in his diet. I obviously reminded the client that this belief has not been proven by science but may be worth a try!

Don't limit the way you receive messages!

Chakras.

I am sure most people are aware of the energy points in the body commonly called chakras. It is generally accepted by most that there are seven basic chakras, or energy centers in the body. Some say less, some say more, but let's focus on the seven most universally agreed upon chakras.

First Chakra – Base Chakra

The base chakra is located at the base of your spine and its color is red. It is generally agreed that this chakra relates to your life in the earth realm. It is what connects you to the earth, besides the less-talked-about ones in the bottom of your feet. When you sit and meditate, this chakra is the closest to the earth. If you have lower back problems, there is an imbalance with earth life. Many times, this is related to money, since we in modern society need money to achieve basic survival. Money buys us food, pays our electric bill, water bill, cable bill, etc. If you grow your own food or live off the grid, then money may not be as much of an issue, but for most people, money is a necessity. Other than money issues, first chakra issues are all about our physical expression of life. Survival and basic needs are first chakra issues.

Second Chakra – Sacral Chakra

Just a few inches above the base chakra is the sacral chakra. It is orange in color and relates to our emotions and connections with others. It is the place where we have sex, procreate, connect with others emotionally, and is generally where our gut instinct lies. Whether we are birthing babies or our next project, it is the creative center of our bodies. Art, writing, music, and any creative expression comes from our sacral chakra. We also connect with others here, so intimate relationship issues are often lodged here as well as in the heart.

Third Chakra – Solar Plexus Chakra

Right around our belly button is our solar plexus chakra. Its color is yellow and it relates to our will and how we relate to the world around us. Where the sacral chakra is more internal, the solar plexus is external. It is our reputation, our sense of self, our ability to show up in the world. If we create a work of art in the second chakra, we offer it to the world in the third chakra. Many would-be artists, musicians, and creators have a wealth of creativity that no one ever finds out about because their third chakra for whatever reason will not allow them to be who they are in the world. On the other hand, many times people who are overly confident, narcissistic, even tyrannical or authoritarian have an over-extended and out of balance third chakra. Many times, this relates to an imbalance between what they feel inside, second chakra, to how they choose to express that, third chakra. What we feel inside and how we act out are often two very different things.

Fourth Chakra – Heart Chakra

Our heart chakra lies directly between the three lower chakras and the three upper chakras and is what connects us all together. There are several colors associated with this chakra, including green, pink and gold, depending on which tradition you follow. Use your intuition to see which color presents itself to you in relationship to this chakra. It is the place of love, both personal and universal. It is where joy and purpose reside. When we lose our sense of purpose or our joy in life, often we have issues in the heart. Our lungs are also directly connected to this chakra, which represents our ability to breathe in life and feel alive. If this chakra is out of balance, our whole life and all of our other chakras are affected. Our breasts are also located near this chakra, which is all about nurturing and being nurtured. Issues with children and parents often show up in the body around this chakra as well as our sacred chakra.

Fifth Chakra – Throat Chakra

Our ability to speak our truth is located in our throat chakra. We also have smaller chakras in our ears and I believe hearing and speaking are related. Blue is the color of the throat and magenta is the color associated with the chakras in our ears. In our ears we often hear words spoken by others that either empower us to speak or silence us. Words contain the power of life and death. Hearing and speaking are intrinsically tied together. If there is an imbalance in the throat, there is often also an intrusion in the ears. We have either heard something that silenced us, or not heard something we needed to hear. A lot of us who have difficulties with speaking our truth have been silenced in some way or have felt not heard. This rarely begins in this lifetime.

Sixth Chakra – Third Eye

Our third eye is the intuitive part of us. It is connected to our inner and outer eyes. Its color is indigo, or a deep purple blue. Many indigenous tribes choose a shaman based upon the eyes. If an eye is damaged or wounded in some way, it is a sign that the person has "the sight". When I was eighteen, I developed a tumor in my left eye. The tumor was removed, but my eyesight never fully recovered in that eye, although I have had some improvement from self-healing. Eventually the left eye veered off to the left. It would be years before I had surgery to have my eye moved back to center. In the meantime, I remember once I went on a vacation to the islands. I was in a local market on one of the islands, and the vendor said to me that I was a star child and had the "sight." I had no idea what he meant at the time. Many times, we intentionally close our third eye, we have it closed for us by others or by our social conditioning, religious beliefs, and our sense of self-preservation. A lot of my clients who have closed their third eye did so out of fear of what they were intuitively "seeing."

67

Seventh Chakra – Crown Chakra

Our crown chakra is what connects us to Spirit, the Divine Presence, or whatever your source is. It is the chakra of Spirit. The colors associated with this are lavender and white. It is what connects us to our own divinity. If we have been wounded by religion or religious leaders, our crown chakra may be affected. When I am channeling spirit, I often feel pressure on the top of my head, not pain, just like I have a weight on the top of my head, or like someone is pushing down on that soft spot on top. When I am meditating, I often will visualize my crown chakra opening up and a light shooting up from inside me while simultaneously the light from above shooting down inside the top of my head through my crown and down through all the other chakras into the earth and then back up.

One of the most effective ways to connect with Source and then to your recipient is to send your awareness up through the top of your head to the Highest Place where Source resides. You will probably feel a shift of some kind. I feel a surge of joy when I arrive there. Then I go back down into my client through the crown chakra. If this chakra is blocked then my first job is to address that and then I continue on into the session.

Hand Chakras

Although not associated with the seven main chakras, we also have chakras in our hands. Not everyone's hand chakras are online, but healers will definitely have active hand chakras. I have never really associated these chakras with a color. My first inclination would be green, since green is the color of health and healing, but there are instances in which green is not appropriate to use when healing, such as when doing work with cancer patients. Green is the color of growth. Cancer is a disease which grows and expands, so I always use purple when doing work with cancer patients or white, which is a universal color and holds within it all colors. Gold or silver also may be appropriate, depending on the situation. Many healers report feeling warmth or a tingling sensation in their hands when healing is needed or sometimes even when they speak of healing. I find my hand chakras tingling while I am writing this book.

Other Chakras

I mentioned we also have chakras in our feet and in our ears, but less talked about are the chakras not located in our physical bodies, but in one or more of our other bodies and that which connects us to the Earth and to the Divine. Some say we have many chakras extending beyond our bodies both up into the heavens and down into the earth. Chakras are energy centers, so I don't doubt this is true. Whether or not we are fully connected to these chakras and whether or not they are activated is another story.

Not all traditions use the chakra system to explain our energy field. I am not going to delve into the Kabbalah and their tree of life or how the indigenous tribes relate to the energy body, since these are not areas I consider myself knowledgeable enough to teach. Whatever tradition you follow, feel free to incorporate your knowledge and understanding of the body and the energy field to your healing practice.

There are also differences between traditions on which chakra holds the core of our soul or is most active. A lot of people assume our soul is located in or near our heart chakra, but I don't always feel it there. Usually when I do an internal scan to see where the core of the light of my soul is, I see it a bit lower, near where the Chinese call the Dan Tien. It feels like it is a bit between the sacral and the solar plexus chakra. As some traditions combine these chakras into one, this makes sense. I have also heard that each of us can trace our origins to different star systems, and we may have the core of our being located in a different place depending on where we originated from. I can't really speak much to this, but it feels right. This would explain why we feel drawn to some modalities, societies, or traditions and not others.

On a more expansive view, our soul is much larger than our human body, and every cell in our body contains within it the DNA of our soul, so who is to say it has to be located in a specific place in our body? Each cell of our body seems to contain a sense of awareness, consciousness, and even memory. When I do healings, I speak to every cell in the body, not just to a core location where the soul seems to be located. My Guides once told me when I asked them "where is the soul" that our soul is everywhere, in our fingernails, in our pinky finger, in our liver, and that was a question that did not really need an answer.

Exercise – Meditating on the Chakras

Close your eyes. Breathe in to a count of 4. Breathe out to a count of 4. Do this until you feel your body relaxing and your state of intuitive awareness becoming more online.

Beginning with your base chakra, imagine your base chakra coming alive with the color red. Imagine a root or a column of light shining down from your base chakra into the Earth Mother to the core of the Earth. Imagine the Earth Mother shines her energy up into your base chakra. If you are standing, you can imagine the smaller chakras in the bottoms of your feet sending the energy down and then back up into your base. Notice the Earth Mother energy make its way up through each chakra, activating each one, shining or spinning out any energetic debris that may be clogging up each chakra. When you get to the crown chakra, imagine your crown opening up on the top of your head and the energy spouting up through the crown, shooting up into the sky and connecting with the Divine. Imagine the energy of the Divine Presence and the energy of the Earth Mother connecting and joining together through your energy centers and empowering you, charging you and activating each chakra.

Write down any insights you receive.

Exercise – Scanning the Energy Field

This exercise is best performed with a partner, but if you don't have one, you can use a pet or someone not in your presence who you have permission to scan.

If you are doing this while in someone's physical presence, ask permission to scan their energy field. Using the aforementioned tools, using your hands, begin several inches away from the body and move closer, slowly, until you feel a shift in the energy field. This could be a tingling in the hands, heat, cold, or other sensations.

If you are not in a person's presence, do the same thing, only using your psychic muscles. See what you see, hear, feel, or have a knowing of when tuning into them. Notice any sensations in your own body when scanning another person's energy field. What do you feel, sense or see? Do you see any congestion?

*I find it helpful to enter the person's energy field and just "look" around. I may feel pressure or pain in my own body which indicates areas of concern in theirs. Or I may enter their energy field through the crown chakra and work my way down, just allowing my psychic senses to pay attention to what I see, feel, hear, taste or smell. A suggestion from Vianna Stibal, who created the Theta Healing Technique * which I really like is to begin at the top and imagine lights turning on as you scan areas of the body. If the area lights up, it is good. If you feel resistance or the light doesn't turn on, that is an indication that there is an area of concern.*

Share what you receive if possible and compare notes. Remember at this point you are just practicing, but if you have healing skills and your partner agrees, offer them the energy of Divine Love or whatever healing modality you feel comfortable using.

Sometimes you will notice brown or black or grey spots or intrusions. Sometimes you may see a scene, like from a movie.

71

Recently I was asked to do a healing on a client I had never met. I received permission, and entered their crown chakra. The brain was completely brown. The left side felt pain, particularly behind the eyes. I saw a black and white movie scene of a cowboy being shot in the head. Immediately I felt coldness all around. I was not completely able to ascertain if the person had been shot either in this life or a previous life, or if he had an attachment of someone who had perhaps been shot. I simply called on the Angels to remove any energy that was not his and heal and resolve the meaning of the vision. I did not receive any specific feedback other than my assessment was spot on.

When my kitty was young, I was tuning into her energy field. I noticed that I only saw blue. Everything that I saw through her eyes was blue! My kitty was colorblind, or so I thought! When I came out of my trance state, I Googled and learned that cats only see in shades of blue and green. She was normal. Apparently, all cats see this way.

It's always nice when something you sense can be verified. It increases your confidence in your intuitive abilities. If possible, see if you can verify any of the information you are intuitively sensing. You can also ask your Guides to give you something you can verify. Not everything can be verified right away, but it is okay to ask for that so you can know you are on the right track.

It is worth mentioning here that if you are working with a partner, it is not necessary for that person to acknowledge what you are sensing! Trust what you feel and sense, whether or not you receive confirmation. It is always nice to get that positive feedback, but the key is to trust your intuitive hits. Many times, in sessions with clients they don't acknowledge some of the information that comes through until later, and sometimes not at all. There have been times that I don't get confirmation until years later.

Suggested Exercises for Chapter Five

Do the suggested exercises as well as continuing the exercises in previous chapters as you are guided.

Journal about your understanding and experiences.

As you go about your day, traveling from place to place, scan the energy in a room and see what shows up for you. Do this frequently until you begin to notice the difference in the ambiance in various locations. As you interact with people throughout your day, notice how you feel when you are in the presence of others. Notice what you notice.

I don't suggest you scan a person's energy field without their permission, but be aware of how you feel when you are around people. Take note of different feelings or intuitive hits and from your heart, send people love who seem to be struggling.

*Vianna Stibal *Theta Healing* copyright 2010 by Vianna Stibal, published by Hay House. THETAHEALING is trademarked and owned by Nature's Path, Inc.

CHAPTER SIX
CHANNELING LIGHT ENERGY

Channeling is when an individual puts aside their own conscious awareness and allows the energy of another being to come into their body to share a message, to heal, or to do other things allowed by the person engaging in the experience.

The biggest question that normally comes up in regards to channeling is whether the person who is channeling spirits is possessed or in danger of being possessed.

I am not sure how others who channel would describe the experience, but, for me personally, I am somewhat aware of what happens and what is said or done, but I am well aware that the information or energy that is coming through is not mine. I know this because I would not have thought of the information on my own or in the case of channeling healing energy, I know I cannot generate healing energy out of the air or just because I want to. Sometimes I can feel a different energy enter my body. Normally I quickly forget what was said or done when the experience is over. I am aware when they have left or if I lose the connection. I am in a bit of an altered state of consciousness, so it is kind of like a dream. If you wake up from a dream, you will be somewhat aware of the dream for a little bit, but if you don't write it down or record it right away, it quickly goes away.

The deeper you are able to go into a trance-like state, the easier it is for the spirit to gain control of the body.

When I am channeling, I am in control somewhat but I am allowing them to use my voice or my hands or whatever. I am putting aside my own consciousness and allowing them to come in. Sometimes it is by intention and sometimes it just happens when I am doing spiritual work or teaching or seeing a client or whatever.

How do I know it is a Higher Vibrational Being and not a ghost or a lower-level entity?

Let's go over three key points in knowing whether or not a message or an interaction with a Spirit is truly from some Divine Presence or perhaps a result of misguided beliefs, a misguided leader, or even a voice from the non-physical world that perhaps is not who it claims to be.

1. Does the message promote harm of self or others?

The Divine or any Benevolent Spirit is not going to instruct you to harm someone or yourself, for any reason. I don't care what the reason is. I am even averse to belief systems that kill animals for rituals, much less humans, although I realize this is the practice in many belief systems. I will admit to eating animals for food, but I normally have the practice of thanking them for giving their life so that I can go on living, and asking that any acts of kindness that I perform that they may share in the reward since some of their life essence lives on in me.

In certain belief systems that do ritual animal sacrifice, they claim that the death is normally quick and as pain-free as possible, and that after the ritual they do consume the animal. They say it is no different than consuming meat, except the death is more humane. I cannot speak to the truth of this claim, since I have never engaged in the practice. Whether or not animal sacrifice is a legitimate spiritual practice is not the subject of this chapter. But harm to self or others is always a true sign that there is some less-than-benevolent spirit interaction involved.

If any communication comes to you from a spirit or by means of psychic transmission of any sort that encourages you or instructs you to harm someone, that communication is not from a Benevolent Presence, despite any claims to the contrary.

75

2. Is the message accepting of those who may believe differently?

The world is full of belief systems who seem to believe that their way is the only way. A lot of these belief systems claim to have received their revelations from a visitation from a Divine Presence. Who is right?

It is not my job to judge whether or not someone is right or wrong in what they believe about the Divine. I am not going to engage in any activity that maligns another belief system, whether that belief system is followed by millions and has been practiced for thousands of years, or has a follower of one. If I have a client who really believes something, and that belief is not hurting them or someone else, I will work with that belief to bring a sense of hope, healing and joy to them. It is not my job to try to change their mind.

3. Is the message in alignment with the law of Love?

Jesus said the only real laws were two: Love God (or your understanding of the Divine), and love your neighbor as yourself. He then went on to tell a story about who constitutes your neighbor, stressing that everyone is your neighbor whether you like them or not. Other belief systems also seem to have this rule. Thus, the third way of discerning whether or not a revelation or message is truly from a Divine Being is to ask yourself, "is this message loving?"

Being a deliverer of messages, I can sometimes agree that not all messages appear on the surface to be loving, but, at the core, really are. Even difficult circumstances many times have positive outcomes. Right before I left the belief system I was raised in, which was my whole life at the time, I received the message that I would be betrayed by a friend, lose everything that held importance to me, and feel lost for a while, but in the end, I would thank the friend for saving my life. That happened exactly as I was told.

Sometimes I use tarot cards to deliver messages. Some of the cards are scary! However, I can say with certainty that I have never told someone a message, no matter how difficult, that did not have some sense of hope or alternative outcome. Sometimes life is hard. Sometimes bad things happen. We can't discount difficult experiences. But I will never tell someone something that is meant in any way to harm them or create sorrow or fear or try to manipulate or control them or extract large sums of money from them. When you were the recipient of a difficult message, was there any sort of solution or resolution or feeling of hope you derived from the message? Did the message inspire you to feel hopeful or hopeless? Love or fear? Freedom or control? Is the person delivering the message going to benefit in a way that is out of proportion to the message?

I never predict deaths, but I may see a difficult experience of loss. I may see the potential for divorce or infidelity, or a need to confront a challenge, but I always leave the decision or any recommended action to the recipient.

Sometimes it is a fine line between delivering a difficult message meant to assist the client to an eventual better experience of life, and giving a message of doom.

If you desire to connect to the higher vibrational beings, remember that your own vibration has to be a match to theirs for there to be contact. It is harder, but not impossible, to channel a Higher Vibrational being if you are mad or sick or depressed. You will normally get the energy that you are a vibrational match to. Now, if an earthbound soul wants to give a message or speak to someone, I have to almost lower my frequency to allow that to occur. Sometimes it is an important aspect of their healing, so I allow it temporarily.

I have read of channels who report being completely unaware of what is going on when they are channeling, but I am not one of those. It is my understanding that this is possible with extremely deep states of trance. I am not completely conscious, but I am somewhat a partner in the process, and can choose to end the session at any time.

When healers, whether it be by Reiki or some other form of hands-on or intentional transmission of healing energy, send healing energy through their hands or through their intention to someone else, they are channeling! They are pulling healing energy from a Power Source, allowing it to flow into their body and out to another person, animal, or other intended recipient.

Many times, when I am doing a healing session, I will feel my Healing Guides coming into my body and I will be aware of the energy flowing out through my hands or through my pendulum or whatever tool I am using. The tools are an extension of the healing energy that is channeling through me to someone else. If it is a message, then it flows out of my voice from the one delivering the message to the person who is receiving it. If someone is there to speak with someone who has passed, often I will feel in my body where they may have had pain in their body. I will feel an impact or a tightness in my body where they had pain in their body, perhaps when they passed or maybe at some point in their life.

As a healer, it is extremely important to build up some sort of ability to channel energy. Everyone's experience with this skill will be different, but allowing the energy of the Healing Guides to use your body to do the work of healing is an essential part of the process. Knowing which tool or modality to use for each individual recipient is also a must.

Years ago, I was teaching a Reiki class. In one of the classes I had a student who was a bit apprehensive of the attunement ceremony. In case you are not familiar, in traditional Reiki, you receive the ability to transmit healing energy known as Reiki by a ceremony in which the teacher inserts into your body the Reiki frequencies. My student in this example had been brought up Christian, and was a bit worried about who or what I was inserting into her body. I was unaware of her concerns when the time came to do the attunements. When I came to her, I felt the presence of Jesus come into my body and felt that it was Him doing the attunement. I felt His hands and his breath and his energy inside of my own body. She is the only student in all my years of teaching where this occurred. After the ceremony, during the time of sharing, I told her of my experience while I was attuning her. She breathed a sigh of relief and then revealed her fears. Obviously, Jesus knew of her fears and the experience eased her reservations and she has now evolved into a wonderfully skilled Reiki healer and teacher.

Channeling is simply setting aside your own conscious awareness, getting into a trance state of some kind, light or deep, whatever your comfort level allows, and surrendering to a Higher Power to come into your body. Most are familiar with the channeling that occurs when spiritual messages come through, but it is also an aspect of performing healings. The Divine Presence comes into our human body, temporarily inhabits our physical form, and does the work.

In Shamanism it is said we are like a hollow bone that the energy flows through. It is important for us to be as hollow as possible when the Divine Presence comes in so that the energy that flows through is pure and untainted by our own shortcomings and human frailties. The Divine Presence uses our form to do the work. We cannot really take credit when someone gets better because we are only the tool that Spirit is using. Spirit needs us to be able to focus and hold a particular frequency so that the link is not broken.

In my experience, sometimes it is possible to break the link and I will feel it when the energy leaves or gets disconnected. Usually this is when my own mind doubts or experiences fear or resistance of some kind. I will admit sometimes when very specific information comes through, a thread of doubt occasionally sprouts inside my head.

"What if this information is incorrect? Are they going to think I am a fraud or a lunatic?"

Confidence comes when we speak out information that comes to us intuitively and the recipient verifies the information. This is called evidentiary information. It is information known to the recipient. In a healing session, this could be something like, "does your neck hurt?" to "are you afraid of not having enough money to support yourself?" or "did your grandmother lose a child?" or any other number of possibilities.

When we are channeling Light Energy to do a healing, it is not completely necessary to receive intuitive information, but when you do receive some information, it is important to share what you get. This will develop confidence in your abilities.

But what if the recipient says, "No, I don't know what you are talking about"?

Stand by what you see! It does mean something.

If I am doing a healing and I see a noose around someone's neck, it is doubtful the person was hanged in this lifetime. It could be something that happened in another lifetime. It could be a friend or family member who hanged himself and is energetically attached in some way to the client. It could be symbolic of an energetic block in the recipient's throat chakra. I normally just share what I see and together, the client and I figure out what it means. I may say, "I see your throat chakra is blocked in some way, and it looks to me like a noose around your neck. Does this mean anything to you?"

Is this all a part of channeling?

Yes!

Where do you think the information is coming from?

Let us do an exercise to bring Light energy into your body. It is not completely necessary to receive any visuals or receive information, but trust the process.

Exercise: Channeling Light Energy

As you have done previously in the other exercises, begin by closing your eyes and counting your breaths for a few moments until you feel relaxed and you notice your awareness is becoming more focused on Spirit and less on your physical body awareness.

Focus your awareness on your heart and begin to feel the emotion of Love. This raises your awareness and your frequency. You can also focus on Joy or Peace. All of these are interchangeable. You could say a mantra, "I now connect with the energy of Love, Joy and Peace." Or simply repeat, "Love. Joy. Peace."

If you have trouble with this step, it is possible that in this lifetime you have not experienced these emotions at their evolved form, so you have nothing to connect the feeling to. This may require some individual work to connect the emotion with your current life experience.

Some like to say the mantra, "I now connect with my Soul."

I find it very powerful to do this exercise in conjunction with the breath. As you focus on the Divine Presence, draw in a breath and imagine the energy of Divine Light coming in to your body on the in breath. On the out breath, breathe the energy of the Divine into your body. This step is optional, but very powerful.

I always seem to notice myself smiling at this point but you may have a very different reaction. This experience should feel good to you. If it does not, there may be some inner healing work you need to do before you will be able to channel Light Energy.

At this point just surrender to the experience. Some report their crown chakras open up and the Light pours down into them from above. Some report seeing a Presence and that Presence walks into their body. In the presence of the Divine, you are safe. Fear will open you up to a less than positive experience, so if you are afraid, please do not do this exercise. Face your fears and release them. Know that the Divine is all knowing, all loving, and only brings a feeling of well-being and Love.

Hold the energy as long as you can. When you come out of the experience, write down any impressions or messages you receive.

Channeling is an important tool when doing healing work because the healing spirits do the work, and if you are adept at channeling them, your healing work takes on a whole new level. This level of healing is tremendously effective, and it is fairly easy! The only thing you have to do is connect with your Healing Guides and witness the healing. They may have you do specific physical things or they may do it all themselves while you watch (intuitively).

I have taught students who have studied energy healing and have not been taught this important step. I am not sure how anyone does energy healing without some sort of concept or understanding of channeling healing energy.

Suggested Exercises for Chapter Six

As you do the exercise to channel light energy, notice what comes up for you in your day-to-day life. How does your life change? As we begin to consciously interact with and channel the energy of The Divine and highly evolved beings of love and light, we will notice our lives changing!

Journal on how you are perceiving your life changing as you are connecting with high vibrational energy.

PART II

SHAMANIC HEALING TECHNIQUES

CHAPTER SEVEN
SHAMANIC JOURNEYING

One of the first things I learned when I became interested in incorporating Shamanic techniques into my spiritual work was the practice of shamanic journeying.

Shamanic journeying is a form of meditation in that it lowers your brain wave frequencies to a level where receiving intuitive information is possible. The difference between traditional meditation and shamanic journeying is that you are actually doing something rather than sitting quietly focusing on your breath or chanting or whatever.

In a shamanic journey you are taking a non-physical journey to the other worlds. This is a joint collaboration between your soul and your imagination. The way you can tell if you are just making it up is that when you try to erase or change something, well, sometimes you can and sometimes you can't. If you are truly in a shamanic trance state, it normally does not occur to you to try to change what you are experiencing, although it can be done, and is sometimes helpful.

There are a couple of basic concepts you will need to know before embarking on your first journey.

The first concept is that of creating a jumping off place that is fairly consistent each time you go. Just as in the previous chapter where I had you close your eyes and imagine the room you were in and then notice what you notice or what you imagine to be there, that room could be your jumping off place. Each time you intend to go on a journey, you would close your eyes and imagine you are in that room.

For me, I call my jumping off place my sacred garden. In it, there is a brick wall all the way around, which creates for me a feeling of being in a safe place where nothing can get in without my knowledge or approval, and a gate with a lock that only I can open. Over time the boundary has changed. In the beginning it was a black wrought iron fence with a gate that had a padlock on it. Over time it has evolved and now my gate opens only when I place my hand on the scanning pad. Hey, technology is not limited to our physical experience. This shows you that you are in charge of your sacred garden, or room, or castle, or whatever you choose.

Inside of my garden, there is a tree that stands in the middle. The tree represents me. The state of my tree symbolizes whatever spirit may want to tell me about my life. There is grass all around, various paths that go to different places, a beach down on one end, and a cave to the right. This gives me endless opportunities to travel into the different destinations in the spirit world.

If your sacred jumping off place is not in a meadow, you will need to create something in that space that represents you. In my garden, the tree represents me but is also a jumping off place. When I enter my garden, I notice my tree and what is happening there. Once my tree was filled with butterflies, which represented a wonderful new beginning. Once there was a man cutting down my tree with a chainsaw! I ran over and got rid of him, but a few days later I was injured in a freak accident. It was only later I realized that the spirit of the chestnut tree I had cut down in my yard may have been mad at me, despite my apologies! No, tree spirits are not always pleasant and easy going! They often get upset with humans and demand payment when we do things that are, in their mind, intruding on their territory. This one played on my guilt. I experienced repercussions from my decision to cut the tree down just because the chestnuts hurt my bare feet and were a pain to pick up. I am not yet sure I have made peace with the angry tree spirit.

It is notable that I was the one targeted, probably because I am aware of the realm of the nature spirits and did not ask permission to cut the tree down.

Some things you can change. Some things not so much. Sometimes the information you see there is predictive, as when I saw my tree being cut down; however, the fact that in my journey I ran over and stopped him before he cut my whole tree down did not stop me from experiencing the accident. Did I make it less severe? Perhaps.

In most shamanic traditions, the practice of repetitive drumming or rattling induces a trance-like state in which intuitive information can be received. I have been able to achieve this state easily with or without the drumming, but everyone is different. Your jumping off place may not be a garden at all. You are the creator of your jumping off place so you get to decide. You can also decide what works for you in inducing the altered state of consciousness. I can achieve it listening to drumming, but I also easily enter a trace state from listening to techno music or the sound of a clock ticking or nothing at all.

Also, in traditional training in the practice of shamanic journeying, you will need to lay flat on the floor or ground and cover your eyes with a cloth so it is completely dark. For me personally, this makes me go to sleep, so I rarely practice this step, but you may want to experiment and see what works for you.

If you have not figured this out already, I am more of a no-rules type of person. Your own spiritual path is yours to follow, and the tools that get you to where you need to be are also going to be different. This is my way. If you are looking for a more traditional way of learning shamanic healing techniques, this may not be the book for you. My number one rule is HARM NONE. If my spiritual practice is helping me and others and it makes me happy, then there is no reason why I should change it just to fit into a box of rules.

Exercise – Take Your First Shamanic Journey

If you are a seasoned in shamanic journeying, feel free to skip this exercise!

In this exercise, you are going to jump off into the world of Spirit!

What you will need:

• *Your choice of background noise: drumming, rattling, music, a ticking clock. Be creative and try more than one tool to see what works best for you! There are shamanic journeying cds and online videos galore! Or you can drum or rattle for yourself, but you won't be able to lie down and cover your eyes if that is the way you want to go.*

• *A place to sit or lie down and a face covering if you want to try that. (I can go on a shamanic journey while running, on some kinds of repetitive exercise equipment, or while doing mundane repetitive tasks!)*

• *At least fifteen minutes of uninterrupted time*

• *A journal to record your experience*

Lie down, sit, or position yourself for this experience. Begin your repetitive sound if you are using anything,

Focus on your breath for a few moments.

Ask your guide or guides to accompany you in this experience.

Imagine you are in a field of grass, or sitting in your favorite meditation spot, or in a castle or a temple or whatever.

You see in front of you a door, or gate, or threshold of some kind that takes you to this sacred place where you will jump off into the world of spirit.

Look around. Notice what you notice. Is there a tree or what is it that will be there every time that represents you? (If your sacred space is inside, you could create a house plant or something that can change in relationship to things you need to know, or you could create a television or movie screen.)

As you evolve in your relationship to your garden, you will notice your garden changing some, but the primary aspects of it will be the same. The cave and the various paths I mentioned before came later. You don't have to create the whole thing right now. Just allow yourself to explore here and notice aspects of your garden.

When you feel the experience is complete, you can bring yourself back to full conscious awareness.

Write down in your journal any experiences you have or any noteworthy details. Some of the details may not mean anything now but will later, so even if something seems insignificant, write it down.

What if you have trouble "seeing" or "sensing" anything?

The following are some common possibilities for trouble doing this exercise:

• Doubt! You could be afraid you are just making it up! Let me encourage you that it is okay to make it up! Your imagination is your doorway into the spirit world.

• You have not entered into the altered state of consciousness necessary to receive psychic information. If you are still in full conscious awareness, you will be unable to receive any intuitive information or be successful in shamanic journeying. It is important to surrender to the experience, and get into that daydream state necessary for this to occur.

• Lack of trust in the spirit world. If you are afraid you are going to connect with demons or the devil or some other non-beneficial spirit, this will stop your ability to be successful. If at this point you are still afraid, you may want to put this book down for a bit and work on your fears.

• Energetic blocks. There are times when for various reasons, there are blocks in your energy field which keep you from entering into the spirit world. It may take some time with your own soul or a healer to discover where these blocks are and how to remove them. (Notice I did not say you have to choose me as your healer. I do personal sessions, but you should find someone you resonate with so that you can have the most beneficial session or sessions necessary to move you to the next level.)

If you have not successfully completed your first shamanic journey, I would move on to some of the other concepts before continuing on here. There are other healing techniques which do not require you to possess this skill. After you have taken your first successful shamanic journey, read on.

The Three Worlds

In Shamanic belief, there are three worlds you can travel to when you go on a shamanic journey. Your first journey is your jumping off place and is actually located in the second world, but it is important to have some idea of where you are going when you travel into the non-physical world.

The first world is the place that is underneath. It is called the lower world. The lower world is symbolic of the subconscious, or that that is beneath the surface. No, it is not hell, although hell is thought to be located beneath us, or in the underworld. It is not a place to fear. If you need to know the answer to a secret, or information that is not out in the open, the lower world may have the answer for you.

In the beginning of my shamanic journeying, I almost always traveled to the lower world. To me there was no other reason to go into the non-physical world other than to receive information that was not known. I traveled there first for myself, and then for others.

Remember that just because it is called the lower world does not mean you are necessarily under the ground. When you go there, you will travel in a downward direction from the jumping off place. This could be a cave, which is how I started, or down the roots of a tree, or any other number of ways. One of my students has a water slide, and she travels down the water slide into the lower world. When you emerge from the feeling of traveling down, you may encounter any number of experiences. That is why you always take a spirit guide with you. Often in shamanic journeying this spirit guide comes to you in the form of an animal, but this does not necessarily need to be the case.

The second world is called the middle world. This is a world that is much like what we experience in waking consciousness, only a little different. This is the place of past, present and future. In my sacred garden, if I am going to the middle world, I go through a door in the trunk of my tree. When I go through the door, I am going to somewhere that looks very much like earth life. If I am going to go to the doctor next week, for example, I may journey to the middle world and have a conversation with my doctor's soul before my appointment so he or she knows exactly what to do or where to focus their attention. You can journey to a potential employer's office before a job interview, to your childhood, to your future self, or any number of other destinations. If you are doing a journey for someone else, you may travel to the middle world to find the source of their problems or to do a healing.

The third world is the upper world. It is the place of spirit, of the Divine, and all things we consider to be above us. Our Spirit Guides and Benevolent Helpers are usually in the upper world. On the flip side, if you or your client likes to engage in mind-altering substances or fantasy of some sort, this is where pieces of their consciousness often get stuck. It is also the place of religious entrapment.

When I go on a journey, normally I don't decide beforehand which world I am going to enter. I allow my guides to decide based upon the reason for my visit. When I approach my tree, I often get sucked up or down or through the door in the tree almost like a vacuum cleaner. Some people have elevators, ladders, steps or any number of ways to go up or down. If you are just getting started in shamanic journeying, you will want to explore all three worlds before you try to heal someone or receive information.

Exercise: Traveling to the Three Worlds

Do the preparation you would normally do to go into an altered state of consciousness. Focus on your breath, call in the Guides, feel the energy of Divine Love and intend your experience will be healing or helpful in some way for yourself or others.

It is not recommended that you journey for someone else without their permission, but if permission is not possible, you can journey to your jumping off place, envision them in front of you, and ask their soul if you can journey for them. You will get a clear yes or no. If you don't receive a clear yes, then do not do the journey. It is unethical to journey for someone without their permission or some sort of permission.

You will first go to your jumping off place. Call in your guides or a guide to accompany you. You may state an intention at this point. For this exercise, the intention is to travel to one of the three worlds.

To increase your confidence, ask your guide to show you something on your journey which you can verify in some way once you return to full conscious awareness. If you see a white lily, for example, the evidence would be to see white lilies in some form or in an unusual way within a day or so after the journey. In traditional shamanism, you would ask to see it three times, especially when the intention is to bring back a power animal. In some form you would see that animal or some representation of it show up for you within a day or so. If you ask to see it three times, then you may want to give spirit a couple days to complete their task.

Only travel to one world at a time during a journey. Come back, return to conscious awareness, and journal about your experience.

Getting familiar with the three worlds is essential to being skilled at receiving information, doing healings, or bringing back pieces of your recipient's life essence. We are starting to get into the meat of doing healing work now. I wanted to cover all the bases and make sure you had the skills necessary to do the healing we will be discussing next.

Suggested Exercises for Chapter Seven

As you embark upon the exercises in this chapter, make sure you are journaling about the information that is coming through for you. If you are having difficulty, write about that! Use your internal magnifying glass and get really close into where the block may be or why you are perceiving having difficulty. Sometimes journaling provides us with insight that comes through as we are writing!

CHAPTER EIGHT

SHAMANIC JOURNEYING FOR HEALING

Life is hard.

Our soul comes into the earth with an overall plan, or life mission. Some call this a soul contract. But we as souls know that earth life is not all that easy, and most of the time we have agreed to forget everything when we get here. Sometimes we get off track or take a detour. Sometimes we experience difficult emotions and find that after a particularly intense experience, we feel a little lost. Some of us come into the world feeling lost.

When we experience an extremely intense event, sometimes a piece of our life essence, or soul, separates from our body and gets stuck in the event or somewhere around the event. Sometimes we lose pieces of our soul to other people or animals. We may love the person or we may hate them, but at some point, we either give them a piece of our life force or they take it. We can lose pieces of our soul to any number of events, or people, or situations. Sometimes we come into life already missing pieces.

As a healer, your job is to help your clients heal. Whether they are coming to you for a physical complaint, an emotional one, or they don't even know why they came, but they just don't feel like themselves, embarking upon a journey to receive information for them can be very healing.

Before you do a journey for someone else, make sure you have been practicing your skills at shamanic journeying for a while.

Hopefully by now you have gained some confidence by asking your guides to give you some verifiable information.

If you have a friend or other spiritual seeker, you may want to practice by doing a journey for them before attempting to heal someone. You are not yet ready to hang your shingle and advertise your healing services, if you even choose to do that. I was fortunate to have a friend who allowed me to practice on her every week for about a year. Even after that I did not charge people for quite some time to do a healing.

Exercise: Do a Shamanic Journey for Someone Else

Begin by finding someone who agrees to allow you to journey for them. In the beginning I would ask verbal permission, but there is a way to ask a person's soul for permission even if you don't have verbal consent. For now, ask permission verbally.

In the beginning, it may be best to be in that person's physical presence. Traditional shamanic training says you should be laying down next to them, and even touching their hand or arm to establish a connection. I can do journeys this way, but these days I don't find it necessary. However, if you are just starting, being in that person's presence will most likely be helpful.

Have the person state their full name out loud three or four times. This aids in establishing a connection with their energy field. Inside yourself, after they have stated their name, you will enter the trance state and intend to go on a journey for this person and bring back helpful information.

This can be done a couple of ways. You can go to your jumping off place, and ask to be taken on a journey for them. Or you can request access to their jumping off place. Everyone has one, whether they use it or not. Sometimes you may begin in your jumping off place and then end up in theirs. You will be traveling to the other worlds for information or to bring healing or helpful insights for them. Ask for information that can be verified or understood by them. You will be taking your guide with you but also most likely at least one of their guides will be joining in.

Allow your guides to lead you into one of the three worlds. Remember that what you see may be literal or symbolic.

In this exercise you will not necessarily be doing a healing, but if something comes up, go with it!

You will be sharing what you receive with your partner after you come back into waking consciousness.

I really only have one rule. You are not going to share information that will make them afraid or predict a difficult event, such as a death or other tragedy. If you received that information, tell them you saw a challenge coming up or word it in such a way that the information is helpful or there is at least a plan of action that can create positive change.

In shamanic journeying, even terrible things are often healing. I was eaten by my power animal more than once. Once my power animal was dead and its dead body was full of maggots. Once my client's tree was on fire. This was not a literal prediction of a fire. Symbolically it represented she was feeling rage. You have to be skilled in interpreting what you see and this comes only with practice.

Soul Retrieval

Soul retrieval is when a healer, using various methods, but in this case, we will be using shamanic journeying, goes into the world of spirit and locates pieces of someone's soul, brings those pieces back, performs a healing on those pieces, and then returns those pieces to the recipient.

I was made aware of soul retrieval by one of my mentors, but I honed the skill by being mentored by a shamanic healer, taking a class from another shamanic healer, and reading books on the subject, only to be told by my Guides not to do it the way I was taught. Nowadays I normally don't even need to go on a shamanic journey to find the lost pieces and return them. Your skills and abilities as a healer will evolve as you acquire more tools. Shamanic journeying is a tool.

In the beginning of my experience with shamanism, I bought a couple of books on the subject and, upon reading a few chapters of the first book, had an 'aha' moment when I "remembered" that I had done it before and knew how to do it. I still felt like I needed to learn from a shaman, so I found some classes and two very different teachers. This is not necessarily the case for everyone.

Finding pieces of people's souls and returning them to their owners is not a practice to be taken lightly or to be taken up by just anyone.

In the early days, I was not taught that the soul may need healing before returning it to the person's body. I was taught that the soul is the purest part of ourselves and has no need of healing. This may be partially true, but the truth is that if the soul escaped the body for whatever reason, there was probably a reason. Most of the time I found the soul had some emotions or limiting beliefs attached to it.

Once I was out running and Jesus showed up for me. I often engaged in shamanic journeys or times of spirit communication while running so I was not that surprised that he had shown up but I was surprised at what he said.

Jesus told me he had a piece of my soul he wanted to give back!

After a little arguing on my part, I agreed to take the soul piece back. I was not aware that my soul might need to be healed first, and Jesus did not tell me. For the next three days I was really pissed off! I got mad at every little inconvenience, every thoughtless driver, every word someone said to me. It took me three days to figure out why I was so mad!

When I left the church, it was not a great experience for me. I had been ordered not to deliver any more "words of prophecy" or messages from Spirit. I was chastised for some messages I had delivered. My best friend betrayed me. All of my daughter's friends were no longer allowed to speak to her. I was mad. I was mad at Jesus. I was mad at his representatives. I was mad at the messages and the gift. I was mad.

When Jesus gave me my soul back, the anger came back too.

This is when I suddenly realized that souls may have some unprocessed emotions and unfinished business revolving around the event that precipitated the fragment happening.

In this case, I was presented with memories revolving around my years in organized religion and the memories of the last moments before I departed that religion. I was forced to address those emotions and given the opportunity to heal them.

I imagine Jesus knew that this was a lesson I needed to learn, and that is why he did not warn me ahead of time or heal my soul before giving it back.

This story illustrates the importance of taking this work seriously! If you are not skilled or knowledgeable in what you are doing, you can do more damage than good!

Other than traumatic events, how is it possible to lose pieces of our souls?

- Other people can steal your soul! Their energy may be attached to the soul piece. This happens when someone has an intense emotional attachment to another individual. This could be as innocent as a mother's love for a child or as malevolent as a stalker or obsessive lover. When a person feels some sort of obsession over another individual, they can intentionally or unintentionally steal a piece of that person's soul.

- Sometimes when we are born, our soul remembers and often longs for whatever we were doing before we incarnated. This is especially true for souls who are somewhat mature or evolved. We may come into life feeling like we are in the wrong place, or there

98

has been a mistake, or we don't belong. In this case, soul loss is a possibility even before our current birth into this lifetime.

• There is also the theory of simultaneous or alternate universes and realities but we won't delve into that rabbit hole right now! Just know there is a possibility that there are versions of you in other times and dimensions.

• Even love sometimes creates the loss of a soul piece. If we really loved something or someone who is no longer in our lives and with whom we cannot imagine living without, we are in danger of losing some of our soul.

• We can lose a piece of our soul in a location, such as a home or any place where we experienced an intense emotion.

One client lost a piece of her soul in a home she had to sell and move out of after a divorce. Her children had grown up here. She had loved the home and all of the precious memories of that home. After moving out, she found herself moving from place to place but never could find a place that felt like home. After bringing her soul back from the house where she left it, she quickly found a home and is still there these many years later. It was important to heal the emotions that created the necessity of her having to move before bringing that piece back.

Can you do a soul retrieval on yourself?

Yes! With your Guides and Spirit Allies, you can fairly easily retrieve a piece of your own soul.

Is it possible to retrieve pieces of your soul from the future?

Once again, yes. I only had this happen once, but I had a client for whom I had done a soul retrieval early on in my practice. Years later she revealed that at the time, the information I had received did not mean anything to her, however, I had written it all down for her. Many years later she found what I had written and was shocked to realize that everything that I had described had happened to her, years after I had originally done the soul retrieval.

You never know when the information will mean something. Don't discount the information you receive just because it does not mean anything to the client at that moment in time. Remember, time does not exist except in our own finite understanding from our perspective here on Earth.

When you give back a piece of a soul to a person who is not present in the session, do they know it?

This may happen when you do a scan of your client's energy field and find a piece of another person's soul in their energy field. You may find it in one of their chakras or floating about in their aura. It is important to return that soul to its owner, and yes, sometimes that person will feel some sort of shift or awareness that something has happened.

Most commonly, that person may feel a disconnect of some sort from your client. They will either feel relief or they may feel a bit of panic if that person is tied to them in an unhealthy way. They may reach out to the client and attempt to reconnect.

Is it ethical to do a soul retrieval on someone who has not given permission?

It depends.

If you are doing a healing session for a client and find a piece of someone else's soul in their aura, is it ethical to leave it there?

I feel it is always ethical to offer healing. The other person may not want their soul piece back. They may try to give it back to your client. They may attempt to reconnect. It is between the client and the other person how they decide to move forward after the healing.

When I discern a piece of someone's soul in a client, I am in the habit of giving that piece to an Angel and letting the Angel decide how to go about giving that piece back to the person who is not present and has not given verbal permission. I also commonly ask the soul of the other person if they want their soul piece back and then I give it back to them when I receive an affirmative response.

How do I do a soul retrieval?

You will go into your shamanic journey as usual. You will state your intention of going to retrieve fragments of the soul of your client. If this is not necessarily your intention, it may occur organically when you are in a journey for someone. If you see little pinpoints or balls of light in specific places or being held by people, this is a good indication that a fragmentation has occurred. Your guides will take you to where you need to be. You will most likely, but not always, receive information that relates to the fragment or where or when the fragmentation occurred. With the help of your guides, you gather up the various fragments, bring them back with you to at least a partial conscious awareness where you can communicate with your client. You can use various healing methods to heal the soul fragment before putting it back in the client's body. If you do Reiki or some other hands-on healing method, this will work. You can also ask an Angel to heal the soul. You will envision an Angel, envision giving them the ball of light representing the client's soul, work with the Angel to heal the soul fragment, and then the Angel can actually place the soul back in the body or you can with your intention, or with your breath or hand gestures.

In traditional shamanism the shaman places the soul back in the body by blowing it into the body in the crown chakra, the heart chakra, and the solar plexus chakra. This is a very powerful way of doing it. When Covid happened, I had to alter the way I did traditional soul retrievals and added in the Angel to do the work so I could position myself at least six feet away from the client, or even to do the work by phone or through various video conferencing platforms.

101

I recently went to a Shamanic retreat and the Shaman in charge did a healing the traditional way by blowing into one of the attendees. Both the Shaman and the attendee ended up contracting Covid. You would think this would not happen when there is so much healing energy flowing about, but obviously it is still a possibility.

In the beginning, all I needed was the clients' permission and name. I would do the journey, write down the information I received, blow the soul fragments into a crystal, and mail the crystal to the client where I would have them sleep with the crystal under their pillow for at least three nights. This still works; I just rarely use crystals for this purpose anymore. You may want to try this if the person you are doing the healing for is not in your geographical area. If you are going to mail the crystal, be sure to assign an Angel the job of getting it through the mail to the recipient. Once a client mailed me the crystal they wanted me to use for the return of her soul, but it came out of the envelope and got lost in the mail before the envelope arrived to me empty. Luckily, I have never lost a crystal after the soul piece entered into it. If you do use a crystal, make sure you have permission from the soul of the crystal to do the work. Use your intuition to receive permission and give the spirit of the crystal a gift in return. I will go into that a bit more later.

You can also employ an Angel to do the return. The Angel actually heals the soul and returns the soul to the body. You are assigning them that job. I often work with the Angels to do the healing and then give them the job of placing the soul fragment back in the body. All that is needed is a sort of collaboration between the Angel and me. Angels do not do anything on their own. They are always in a dance with us. In the Earth realm, we are working as a team with the Angels and the Benevolent Healing Spirits when doing healings.

Nowadays I see clients in person and also by phone and Zoom and have successfully returned pieces of their soul despite their location. Time and space do not exist in the world of Spirit.

Now I find it is a valuable experience for the client to be involved in the process when the healing is occurring, if this is possible. I like to do the healing and then have them breathe in and welcome their soul back into their body. Give them a few minutes to sit in the present moment and enjoy the experience.

If you plan on doing a soul retrieval for yourself and you know where the soul fragment is, or who has it, you can do a version of a shamanic journey. Go to your sacred garden, surround yourself with your Angels, Guides, and Power Animals, and envision in front of you the translucent Angel that stands between you and the person who has your soul piece. Say to them that you are requesting your soul piece back. They may willingly oblige or they may protest! Either way, they have no choice. It is your soul piece. Imagine them holding a ball of light in their hands and giving it to the Angel. The Angel heals the soul fragment and places it in your body. Breathe in deeply and welcome the soul fragment back into your body. You may also want to do an internal scan and make sure you do not have a soul fragment from this person. If you do, give the soul fragment to the Angel and say some words, such as, "I give you back your soul piece with the help of Divine Love." The Angel is responsible for healing the soul fragment and giving it back to the person. You can do this as many times as necessary for as many people as you feel may have a soul fragment. You can do this whether or not you know who has the soul fragment. You may be surprised to find fragments of your soul coming back from various people, places, and situations.

You don't have to know all the details surrounding the soul loss. Every day I connect with my soul and send a beam of the light of my soul up to the Creator. Recently upon connecting with my soul, I noticed the light of my soul was missing some pieces. I sent out an intention and a call to all the pieces of my soul which were missing from my body to come back and be reunited with my physical body. I imagined the pieces getting healed and then I imagined them coming back into my body. I have no idea where they were or how long they were gone. I just happened to notice they were missing!

I recently listened to a channeled recording of one of my mentors, **Christen McCormack*** as she channeled Archangel Michael and he said that all that was necessary was to run the soul piece through the energy of Divine Love and Joy and it automatically healed any unhealed emotions that may have kept that piece fragmented. I see this as visualizing a sort of shower of Divine Love and Joy and watching as the soul piece gets a bath and then putting it back in the recipient.

After this is over, you may want to seal your energy field with love. The other people involved are not your responsibility to heal. Let the Angel decide how to deal with those individuals.

You can do this method for yourself or someone else. Remember that when you remove energy from yours or someone else's energy field, you need to refill that empty space with the light of your soul or Divine Love, or both!

*When should we **not** do a soul retrieval?*

• You should not do a soul retrieval if the person has not given permission.

Often, I have mothers who want me to do a soul retrieval for their children. I will go into an altered state of consciousness and ask their soul's permission, but if the answer is no, I will not do it.

Once I did a shamanic journey for a man in a coma. Obviously, he could not give permission. When I entered the trance state, I found him and asked permission. He told me he was having trouble leaving the earth plane because of his grieving wife. She had not left his side in weeks, even to sleep or shower. He showed me a picture of them ballroom dancing together. I spoke to him and told him it was really his decision to stay or go and she would be okay. I spoke to her soul and encouraged her to give him permission.

SACRED PATH TO WELLNESS

Soon after I did the journey, he woke up. He sat for a bit with his wife. Then he went back to sleep and passed quietly. The wife later revealed that they met while ballroom dancing and that it was very meaningful that I had given her that detail.

• Do not do a soul retrieval when a person does not want to be in their body.

When someone is regularly self-medicating with drugs, legal or otherwise, they are willingly leaving their body. Never do a soul retrieval on an active addict. Addicts, on some level, do not really want to be here and are self-medicating to take them out of their body. If you return pieces of their soul, they will often get worse. A person needs to be in agreement that they want to be here, alive and well in order to do any sort of healing on them.

I find many lightworkers who are not completely in their bodies. Many of them don't want to be here. I am not sure if their souls just remember the other side or experience ecstasy while out of the body either during spiritual experiences or meditation or from other experiences. It is important as a healer and a lightworker who agreed to be here in the earth realm before you incarnated to be in your bodies. Your body is what connects you to the earth realm and it is where you agreed to be in some way. You may temporarily leave your body while in altered states of consciousness, but you need to be awake and aware and be experiencing some sort of connection to your body and your earth life to be a skilled healer. As a healer, we are joining with the Divine and bringing healing into the physical realm. If we are not grounded in our bodies, we cannot correctly channel healing energy to others.

Remember the paramount rule of permission and free will when doing any spiritual work. Never assume you know what the person's highest good is. We don't know.

Recently I was assisting a family find their runaway teenage daughter. At some point I did feel I was interfering with her free will at the moment and stepped back a bit. I told her family to hold a picture of her and let her soul know they loved her. My work consisted of attempting to align her soul with her highest good without being attached to a particular outcome. She was found about a week after her disappearance. In no way am I taking credit for finding her, but I attempted to afford her the space to make her own decision and align with her highest good.

•   Many times, as healers, we desire to be of assistance to people we love, but often this is not a good idea. Family and close friends are often another group of people you should steer away from doing soul retrievals for. I am not saying I have not done it, but sometimes a healer needs to be a bit more objective than you can be if you are involved emotionally in the outcome.

•   Be sure to be the human vessel doing the work but carefully follow the instructions of your guides. Some times the soul is not ready to heal and there will be resistance. Allow the guides to tell you what they need. Sometimes there are outside forces that seem to be interfering in the healing process. We will discuss that later.

Exercise – Soul Retrieval

The first time you do this, you should find someone safe to practice on. I know I said close friends and family members may be a red flag, but you have to practice on someone! I practiced for a year on a friend. I did not do a soul retrieval each time, but definitely more than once.

Traditional shamanism states you should never bring back more than three fragments at a time. It can be a bit of an overload to get too much at once! I use this as a guideline but not a hard fast rule. Sometimes I get one. Sometimes more. The guides know what they are doing so I normally let them decide. I know when they are done.

Using the techniques described, with someone's permission, go into a shamanic journey for them with the intention of finding a lost piece or fragment of their soul. Be open to going in to one of the three worlds. Take your guides with you! Allow them to do the work.

Come back into at least partial conscious awareness and allow your guides to tell you how to return the soul back into the body, using the previous examples. Make sure the soul is healed before placing back into the body.

Share with the client any information you received. Make sure they welcome the piece of their soul back and take a few moments to sit in the present moment and allow their body and soul to shift.

After a soul retrieval, it is important for the client to be fully in their body. Some sort of physical movement is a good idea, or eating or drinking something.

It is possible for the returned fragment to leave again if the reason why it left in the first place has not been resolved! It is important to chat with the client about the trapped emotions, limiting beliefs, or circumstances which led to the fragmentation in the first place. It can be detrimental to a person to bring back a piece of their soul before they have identified and healed the reason for the loss. Sometimes they have a habit of acting or thinking which needs to be shifted for there to be lasting change.

Sometimes people have lived with a trauma or version of themselves for so long they do not know who they are without it. It took me two years after leaving the church to find some portion of myself I recognized without the umbrella of my belief system. Healing is incremental.

Soul retrieval is not a one-time-fix-all solution.

Treat soul retrieval with reverence and caution. Remember the rule of three. What you do will be visited upon you three times. I would be very choosy about when, how and even if to incorporate soul retrieval into your healing repertoire.

Exercise to try at home.

Other than the previously suggested exercise on soul retrieval, you can practice on yourself!

Go into an altered state of consciousness and go to your jumping off place. Call your healing team: angels, guides, power animals, ascended ancestral healing spirits, ascended masters or whoever you connect with who is benevolent and highly evolved in the spirit world.

You may know exactly when and where you lost a piece of your soul, but be open to going on a journey to find your own soul pieces that are separated from you. You may find the ones you are expecting, but you may also find you lost pieces of your life force in forgotten times and places.

When you find the soul pieces, which look to me like mini balls of light, heal them in whatever way feels good to you. Give them to your healing team, hold them in your hands and channel healing energy into them, or run them through a shower of Divine Love and Joy.

Breathe in and feel the soul pieces come back into your body.

Say, "Welcome Home."

Suggested Exercises for Chapter Eight

You have been given a lot of work to do and exercises to try with this chapter. Take your time! If you don't feel ready, it is perfectly acceptable to take a break, go back to working on a previous chapter, or spending as much time as you need on this chapter. You can even skip this chapter if it seems too intense.

Make sure you are journaling about your progress, your thoughts about the process, and how you are feeling changes happening within yourself and in your lifestyle and daily activities.

It is normal to begin to notice subtle changes in your day-to-day life. Your eating and sleeping habits may change. You may gain or lose weight. You may feel led to eliminate some toxic behaviors or patterns.

Take a moment to do a bit of self-evaluation at this point.

Christen McCormack; www.christenmccormack.com

CHAPTER NINE

SHORTCUTS TO OTHER DESTINATIONS
IN THE NON-PHYSICAL WORLD

I mentioned previously that my sacred garden had various paths going to different places and a cave off to the right. Let's talk about some of the paths that you can add to your jumping off place. Feel free to experiment with these various paths and see which ones speak to you. Not all of these are specifically shamanic, but you can access many worlds by starting at your jumping off place.

1. Akashic Records

In my sacred garden there is a path that leads to the Akashic Records. This is a giant library in the upper world that is often talked about in many belief systems under different names. It is a place where the records of all lifetimes of all souls are kept. You can access the Akashic Records by creating a path there, or you can simply take a journey to the upper world and ask your Guides to take you there. You could create various doors in your jumping off place, with a door that leads there.

Intention to go there is really the only necessity to accessing the records. When we are not in physical form, journeys really only take intention. As soon as you think or intend to go somewhere, you are immediately there. The time it takes to get there or the path you travel to get there is really not an issue.

For me, I have a path. As I am walking the path there is a door with three gatekeepers. The gatekeepers let me in because they know me. On the other side of the door there is another path. At this point the path is mostly white and there is a bridge that leads to a beautiful park-like setting. The grass is green and off to the right there is a lovely manicured pond. There have been times before I created the path or in other forms of meditation, I have found myself rising up through the middle of the pond and finding my Spirit Team there waiting for me. We often sit there in a semi-circle and have chats. Sometimes I end up in this park and we have celebrations where there is dancing and I find all my spirit team and many times friends and relatives who are passed joining in the celebration.

Beyond the park there is a large expanse of beautiful buildings with marble stairs and a huge veranda. As you walk up the stairs you are greeted by a guide of some sort. This does not necessarily have to be one of your own guides, but normally an akashic records guide. You tell the guide why you are there and he or she opens the door.

Your experience beyond this point is your experience. For me, there is a large foyer with hallways and stairs and elevators. The guide takes me to my room or whoever I am accessing the records for. As I enter the room the information I am requesting is there in some form, either symbolically or on a movie screen or in a book or even on another path to another place.

Accessing Akashic Records is not complicated or difficult. You don't even have to see the building! You could open the door and be where you need to be. I just enjoy the journey. Sometimes I see different things along the path that are important. Sometimes I end up at the park and never move beyond that.

Accessing this place is good for healing because sometimes there is information there that is helpful to a client in resolving unknown or misunderstood issues. It may give a client a sense of their purpose in life or reason for being here. It can guide them in knowing when a shift has occurred or if there has been a change in their soul's status or mission. Sometimes we complete our purpose way before the end of our life and we as a soul decide to embark upon additional adventures or missions. Sometimes we may decide to abort a mission and shift directions. All of this information is accessible in the Akashic Records.

2. Past lives.

Yes, you can access past lives by creating a path that leads you to a past life or by going to your tree or elevator or whatever you have in your jumping off place and asking to be taken there. If you are using an elevator, the door would open, you would enter through the door, where there is another back door which opens and takes you to your past life. The middle world normally takes you to past lives on Earth, but if you have lived lives in other dimensions, on stars or planets, or universes, the upper world will take you there. I once went into the upper world and found myself on one of Saturn's rings and another time I had crash landed on Venus. Don't discount any of your experiences and be open to whatever occurs. You may be a beggar, a king, a famous person from history or an alien being or anything in between. No, we weren't all Napoleon or Joan of Arc but perhaps if you access their lifetime, you will access some information that can be verified or that is something you need to know.

Here is my thought on past lives. Accessing them is not for entertainment necessarily. I find a lot of people who are interested in knowing who they were in a past life. My reason for accessing them is to bring healing or closure to an issue in a current life. If you lived a life, died at peace with no unresolved issues, that life is probably not the one that will come up for you. If a lifetime comes up, it is probably because there is something there which was unresolved that needs to be addressed so you can find healing and move on.

I once saw myself on a Viking ship having my tongue cut out. In my younger days I was very shy and would never speak. This limited my socialization abilities and my career choices. Nowadays I am a spirit communicator, teacher, and even wedding officiant. When I accessed the lifetime where I witnessed my tongue being cut out, I actually did a redo. I went back to that lifetime and created a very large man standing behind me which averted the whole incident. I can't specifically say that after this healing I was immediately cured, but now I am not plagued by bashfulness or the inability to speak. Most of the time when we facilitate a "redo," we will notice improvement over a period of time. It is not always immediate.

Naysayers may argue that I made up in my imagination the vision of having my tongue cut out. I can't say for sure, since it is a past life and I did not receive any evidentiary information. The experience felt very real and healing occurred. I maintain it does not matter.

3. River of Life and Ocean of Divine Love.

In *Holy Fire® Reiki**, there are several places where you go or take your client to let them experience healing or receive it yourself. I will not go into a lot of detail here based on copyrights and such, but as a Holy Fire Reiki Master Teacher, I have access to these places. It is no surprise that I would have created paths in my sacred garden that lead to these places.

4. The cave of quarantine.

This technique I learned from shamanic teacher *Christina Pratt**. If you want detailed teaching on this technique, you can access her online class on the *Shift Network**. The purpose of the cave of quarantine is to put various unwell ancestors there who may be creating disharmony in your or a client's energy field, but who are unwilling or unable to heal or cross over. The short version is that you create a cave, assign an Angel or helping spirit to stand guard and create a sort of jail cell for deceased, unwell ancestors who may be interfering with your or a client's ability to heal.

I will be teaching an alternative method for dealing with unwell entities which does not interfere with any copyright laws as far as

I am aware. I don't use the cave of quarantine that often, but it is helpful if I find that I am unable to help heal a deceased ancestor and repair the imbalance any other way.

Suggested Exercises for Chapter Nine

Take four journeys into your sacred garden or jumping off place and create paths to the Akashic Records, Past Lives, the River of Life and/or Ocean of Divine Love, and the Cave of Quarantine. If you are not familiar with these places, all the better! Allow your connection to your team of spirit helpers make these experiences real and specific to you!

Journal about your experiences!

* *Holy Fire Reiki*®, https://www.reiki.org

Christina Pratt, An Encyclopedia of Shamanism, www.whyshamanismnow.com; www.lastmaskcenter.org

*The Shift Network, https://theshiftnetwork.com

CHAPTER TEN
EMPLOYING HEALING SPIRITS

There is a Shamanic technique for requesting a healing spirit to work in tandem with a natural object like a feather, crystal or stone in order to be used as a tool for doing healing work.

This also works with manmade objects! I have done ritual to connect all of my healing tools with a higher form of awareness or power. I even empowered a dollar bill and placed it inside of my wallet to be used as a tool of protection over my finances. Sometimes if my clients feel their life is in danger, I will create a protection item for them by using the following method. Remember that anything that facilitates a feeling of well-being is a tool for healing. As stated before, this method does not replace conventional methods for healing or protection, but are simply an added tool to enhance a state of well-being.

The following method is to increase the power of an object of healing so that the object has some sort of conscious agreement and awareness of the work that is being done.

Every action has a consequence. It seems that the more aware you are, the more you are called to account for your deeds. When employing a spirit to work with you and a particular object, it is important that your motives be pure and that you have the conscious agreement of the spirit you are employing.

I once put a man's name who was extremely difficult in an envelope and wrote Reiki symbols all over the envelope hoping to keep him from being such a difficult person (this was not my first word of choice). The next morning, I heard his soul screaming at me to let him out. I refused. I went ahead and went to work where I walked in the door and immediately received disciplinary action for an insignificant transgression that I could not disprove.

What was my mistake? My intention was not his highest good. My intention was to change his basic personality without his permission. I did not care that his soul said no.

It is really, *really* important to do healing work with the permission not only of the recipient, but of the tools being used, the spirits being employed, and even the land upon which you are doing the healing.

In Shamanism it is believed that *everything* has its own form of consciousness and free will. The chair upon which I sit is made from material that originated from some sort of plant or animal, and other ingredients of unknown origin. It also contains the energy from its creator, any machines which aided in its assembly, and everyone who had a hand in its manufacturing. It contains the energy of its color and the tapestry that covers it. And it has its own sense of purpose. And it contains some of my energy, because here is where I sit when I meditate, when I write, and where I see clients.

A feather contains the energy of whatever bird it was attached to, to the spirit of air and earth (birds have to land and build their nests somewhere!) to its own sort of conscious awareness, and to spirit. Rocks and crystals and any natural objects carry with them the collective consciousness not only of the earth, but of the location where they originated, of the happenings around them, of the spirits in charge of locations, and much more. They seem to retain the memory of everything that has happened around them. Many times, when I touch a tree intending to access its wisdom, I will see images that are not at all natural. I see happenings in the world around them, and even in distant locations!

Healing spirits come in all forms and varieties. You don't have to know details really except to know that they have a form of conscious awareness and need to be in agreement with their essence being put inside the object.

The first step would be to choose a feather or other object. You will need to ask the object to be used as a healing tool. You also need to offer a gift in exchange for its services.

Offering gifts to items from nature and to helping spirits is an often-overlooked aspect of doing magical or healing work. Obviously, in organized religion it is a well-known aspect of church to give offerings of money and service to others but sometimes the practice has been abused. In my way of offering gifts, it is the spirits or nature who benefits.

What are some suggested or acceptable ways of giving gifts to spirits or objects from nature?

Apples seem to be my favorite gift to spirits. I often give gifts of apples when requesting good weather or to appease nature spirits. Sometimes they also like chocolate, wine, money, or herbs. Indigenous tribes often offered cornmeal or tobacco; however, from my perspective, perhaps this is because these items were important to their culture at the time. They seem to like things that mean something to us. Don't give them old fruit you were getting ready to throw out anyway. They *will* be offended. If you are out in nature and find a stone or herb you want to harvest or take home, and you don't happen to have an apple with you, it is acceptable to offer them a gift of your hair, or spit, or some of the water in your water bottle. However, I find this only works if you promise to offer a better gift when you get home. I often offer to send Reiki into the earth, pick up trash I find along the path, or to give to charity. This works depending on the spirit. Sometimes they are happy just to be asked. Most people don't think to ask.

You will need to get permission from both the healing tool and the healing spirit that has agreed to be used for healing work, and gifts should be offered to both.

After you have gotten permission and offered a gift, hold the object in your hand.

You will begin by creating a sacred circle and standing in the middle. Open ceremony in your way, but you can use the ceremony I shared in the previous chapter of calling in the directions if that speaks to you.

Holding the object in your hands, in prayer position, call upon the spirit of the object and the healing spirit which are joining forces to be used as a tool for healing.

Breathe in, imagining the forces of the directions coming in to your body either simultaneously or in turn. You can face each direction in turn, breathing in the energy of that direction, or you can face the direction that speaks to you, possibly in tandem with your intended use for the object. (In my way of understanding, North is wisdom and is associated with earth. East is air and is associated with illumination and new beginnings. South is fire and is associated with movement, growth, and change. West is water and is associated with emotions and letting go. If none of these seem to fit, face north.)

With your eyes closed, imagine Divine Light and Power coming in to your body from the seven directions, both through the top of your head and into your heart. On your out breath, imagine you are blowing up a balloon of energy inside your heart chakra. When your intuition tells you that the energetic balloon is full, with your breath, blow into your hands where the sacred object you have chosen is resting between your palms. Imagine the helping spirit entering the object and the object is awakening and allowing this joining to occur.

You can speak words that invite the energies to become one and to be awakened or you can do this all with your inner vision. Either works.

In other traditions this is an acceptable practice, and many talismans or fetishes are ignited in this way. You can also do this regularly for your own spiritual ignition and empowerment. I would like to give credit the source of this information, but I have found it in various traditions and books with slight variations, and I combined some of the techniques into my own way of doing it, so you will probably not find this exact way done elsewhere. Maybe you will.

You will probably feel a difference in the object. Your hand may tingle or shake. Everyone feels the energy differently.

Another way to awaken the object is to go on a shamanic journey to your sacred garden or jumping off place. Contact the spirit of healing and the object and ask if they would be willing to be used as a tool for healing. After you have received an affirmative response, allow them to join forces while in the journey. Be led by your guides and their energies as to how to proceed.

Now, you will use this tool to bring healing!

It is important to honor the spirits by placing the object or tool in a place of respect either on your altar or a specific location. Periodically give the spirits gifts of thanks.

If at some point in the future, you would choose to discontinue using the object for healing, or feel led to release it and the spirit from its contract, you can take the object out in nature and bury it in the ground or release it in a moving body of natural water. On a windy day, you could take it outside and allow the air to take it away from you. Make sure you thank the object and the spirit for its service to you.

How do you use your chosen tool for healing?

I use Feather to comb my energy field or others who come to me in person. I use it to scan energy fields for imbalances or to do psychic surgeries. I use crystals or stones to pull energy out of clients or flow healing energy into clients by allowing the client to hold the object or by placing on their bodies. I use pendulums for many healing techniques which I will share in a future chapter. I also empower my tarot cards and other items and each has its own unique purpose. Sometimes I will place an object in a location and give it a specific job.

In the case of Feather, beginning at the top of the head, work your way down your person's energy field front and back. If you feel an intrusion, use it as a psychic knife to dig it out. Do so very gently and ask the angels to apply any necessary psychic anesthesia.

After removing any energetic blocks, you can give it to the angels, release it into the earth, or have an empty bowl on hand to put it in to be discarded later. I have only found it necessary once to use the bowl technique and take it outside later and release into the actual earth. In my healing room, I have several plants and many times I release energetic debris into the dirt. They actually like it! It is like giving them fertilizer.

Remember when you remove something out of someone's energy field it is important to fill up the hole! I like to fill it up with Divine Light or the energy of the client's higher self or soul.

After I have done a healing like this, I like to close the session by circling them with the rattle four times. I do this when finishing up many healing sessions. I was taught to close a session with a rattle by my Shamanic mentor **Susan Wolf*** and it feels good when I do it. I think rattles or other objects that create sound are very healing and, combined with my intention, is a way to indicate to the spirit world that the session is complete. It also creates a force field around the client that protects their energy field while the healing is integrating.

My number one rule is that anything you do must be done with love and with the intention that the highest good for all parties involved be done. There is no taking spirit hostages or causing harm allowed. As I mentioned before, doing this ritual for anything other than the highest good for all is possible but not beneficial.

Sometimes it can be a temptation to do spirit or magical "spells" or rituals when someone is causing harm or behaving badly, or even if they have maligned you or made you mad. Remember that everything you do has consequences. It is best to allow the Justice of the Universe to take revenge or to allow consequences for bad actions. Taking that responsibility upon yourself is neither wise nor beneficial. Employing a spirit to assist you in doing these things is extremely dangerous and the results are never good.

Suggested Exercise for Chapter Ten: Empowering An Object

For this exercise you can choose an object of your choice to empower and request for it to be used as a tool for healing.

Connect with Source Energy in the way that speaks to you.

With your breath, pull in the Energy of the Divine into your body.

Make the request for a healing spirit to join with the spirit of the object to be empowered to be used as a healing tool.

You can blow the Divine Breath into the object, or face each of the directions and make your request, whichever method feels good to you. In the beginning, you may want to try both methods and see what feels good to you.

As suggested, you may also want to try to do a shamanic journey to empower an object and see how that feels to you.

Empowering objects are common to many different spiritual traditions.

Always do this in tandem with the spirits with the intention that the highest good be done for all concerned.

Thank the spirit and the object for its service.

Offer appropriate gifts to both the spirit and the object.

Journal about your experiences.

Susan Wolf www.healingwithsusanwolf.com

CHAPTER ELEVEN

ASSISTING EARTHBOUND SOULS THE SHAMANIC WAY

In the beginning of my exploration of various spiritual paths, the only exposure I had to the subject of depossession was in Pentecostal circles. I knew how born-again Christians cast out spirits. When I left that belief system, I pretty much threw the baby out with the bath water. I decided I didn't really know if demons or devils even existed, and I had no desire to find out. In my version of born-again Christianity, we did not believe in ghosts or souls who did not cross over in some way. When you died, you either went to heaven or hell. There were only two options. And if something bad was happening, it was probably the devil making it happen.

Fast forward several years. I had moved beyond the faith of my early years and, in the process of my awakening, was introduced to shamanism. I spent much of my time searching online for various classes. I had taken the prerequisite classes necessary to explore some deeper and less talked about shamanic skills within the tradition I had found. A class popped up in my radar called "Depossession". I was intrigued. Without hesitation, I signed up.

I was astonished to hear the very first words spoken by the teacher, Dana Robinson*, who taught under the umbrella of the *Foundation for Shamanic Studies.*

All spirits are handled with love.

What!!

Handling less than benevolent spirits with love had not been my experience in Christianity. Nor was it the practice on television or in movies. I could not imagine how love was going to do the trick, but I was immediately hooked.

In this particular version of shamanic teaching, devils or demons or the idea of the devil was not really addressed except to say that most of the time, malevolent acts or activity were earthbound spirits, not demons. We treat them with love. We give them a voice to speak their reason for not moving on, and we convince them to go to the light.

This is done through the use of a medium, another person who acts as a questioner or therapist for the spirit and a loving circle of community.

It is the belief in many indigenous tribes that community and a sense of belonging is often what is missing when a soul goes astray. Offering the lost soul what they are lacking and convincing them that they are loved is what they need to find their version of the light.

The White Table

In order to do a depossession in this tradition, the suffering individual is brought into some sort of community gathering. The community holds the circle of healing energy and the medium or mediums begin to bring through the lost soul or souls who are agitating or acting through the living person.

This is when the medium has to trust the community and the community's responsibility is to hold the space for the medium so he or she is safe and is in no danger of the earthbound spirits deciding not to vacate the medium. The person who is being agitated by the spirit or spirits also has to desire to be healed. Sometimes this is not necessarily the case.

In some traditions, everyone wears white and sits around a white table. Salt is poured in the four corners and offerings are given to the helping spirits.

The medium goes into an altered state of consciousness and begins to bring forth information about the earthbound soul. (I am using the "she" pronoun here for the medium and "he" for the earthbound soul but the genders can be male or female) The medium normally feels the earthbound soul's energy enter her body. She may feel pain where the soul felt pain. She may feel the emotions he was feeling at the time. She may see what he saw, heard what he heard, or be thinking what he was thinking.

The medium will begin to allow the earthbound soul to use her voice to speak. The questioner or therapist will begin to ask him questions, like, "What do you see?" "What is happening?" in order to begin the conversation.

The goal is to help the earthbound soul to realize that it is not in his best interests or in the interests of the living to be in this in-between situation. Sometimes it is necessary to help him move past a traumatic event, such as his death or the death of a loved one. Many times, they attach to living souls who are grieving their death. Sometimes they don't know they are dead. Sometimes they are looking for someone, or continuing to experience a high from an addiction through being attached to another addict. Sometimes they attached to the light of someone's soul who was close by at the time of death, mistaking their light for "the Light." Sometimes souls are piggybacked on other souls. The only way to know for sure is to give them the opportunity to speak. The questioner's job is extremely important, because he is the one who convinces the earthbound soul to look for the light.

When the earthbound soul realizes that it is in his best interests and the interests of the living to move on, he normally goes to the light fairly quickly. The angels, helping spirits, and loving ancestors are there to assist him to the light.

When a soul moves on to the light, I normally feel an intense sense of joy well up from inside of me like a fountain. It is an extremely enjoyable event. Normally all participants feel some sense of relief or extreme well-being.

It is not completely necessary to have a person be in attendance to whom the ghost is attached. On more than one occasion I have hosted these events at my home where I invited a chosen group of people who I trust to sit in circle with me and offer this service to any earthbound spirits who are ready to tell their story and cross. The helping spirits bring them to us and we give them space to feel loved and safe to move on.

If any gifts have been offered to the helping spirits, they need to be given to the earth after the ceremony and the space cleared.

The Rainbow Bridge

Another way to assist earthbound souls to the light is called the Rainbow Bridge.

The rainbow bridge is a bridge that joins the world of the living to the world of the dead. You can cross over lost souls in this way either by yourself or in a group setting. In your altered state, you would envision a rainbow bridge which joins the world of the living to the after world. You would call in your helping spirits and loving ancestors, both yours and the loving ancestors of the deceased to line the sides of the bridge and offer the lost soul community and support.

Offering earthbound souls an opening to cross over is often all that is required to help them cross. This can be used for those who are fairly easy and ready to cross. You can say a prayer of some kind sending them love and helping them to release their suffering.

Christina Pratt in her series on healing with Well and Unwell Ancestors on the Shift Network has some amazing prayers and protocol for performing this ritual. Without infringing on her teachings, I would simply suggest creating a prayer that addresses their concerns and offers them hope and healing. (See footnotes in Chapter Nine.)

Do all indigenous tribes believe that activity that is dark in nature is the work of earthbound or lost souls and not necessarily conscious energy that is devious or evil?

I am sure there are many traditions who address protocol for handling non-beneficial energies who are not necessarily earthbound souls in a shamanic way, but in my path of learning, I have not really come across it. I will address how I do it in a later chapter, but the greatest lesson I want you to take away from this chapter is that everything we do, we do with love. We love the living. We love the dead. We love all forms of conscious awareness whether they are nice or not. We do our work with love as our main tool.

We do not yell at ghosts. We do not threaten them or set up reenactments of their deaths to get them to manifest. We do not remind them of their worst moments or invite them to manifest in devious ways. We do not cast out spirits without thought of where they go after we cast them out, thus allowing them to continue in their suffering or posing a danger to other living souls who happen along their path.

We treat the dead with love and respect in the same way we would the living. They also have free will; however, their free will cannot interfere with the free will of the living. If the living do not want them around, they do have to go. They do not have to go to the light if they don't want to, but they cannot stay attached to the living if the living do not want them there.

I think sometimes we put too much emphasis on binding or casting out the demonic and too little emphasis on love and our own vibrational energy field.

If we are living lives of love, joy and peace, it is doubtful that we will be a magnet to dark energy. In my experience of visiting places where people report hauntings or scary activity, when I begin my walk-through, I often find difficult emotions attached to the living, especially if it is a family home. If the living residents are fighting, grieving, or depressed, if they are engaging in frequent drug use or maybe they are ill, their life force is at a fairly low frequency. That is like a porch light to a moth!

Yes, it is sometimes the case that a location can have the energy of the dead there, or a difficult emotion could have gotten stuck there. Normally a fairly happy individual or family will pass up the opportunity to move in to a location like that. Something just won't "feel right."

We are magnetic souls and we will attract the energy that we are an energetic match to. If we are sad, we will attract more sadness. If we are fearful, we will attract more reasons to be afraid. If we are happy, we will attract more happiness.

We are what we think about most of the time. Sometimes those thoughts are conscious, and sometimes not so much. We will deal with some of that later. However, I want to address the slice of the population who seems addicted to death and fear.

I don't like to focus all of my attention or practice on helping lost souls or removing dark entities. It is important to be in the light more than you are in the darkness. That is why I am separating my sections on this aspect of healing work. If you do this type of work all of the time, you will begin to become out of balance.

Also, if you learn a new skill, it seems that you will be immediately called upon to use that skill, at least that is how it works in my own experience. It is almost like my Guides want to offer me practice time for my new skill so they send people my way who need that particular skill. If you are not energetically up to the task, you should probably stay away from this sort of work.

If you do choose to assist the unwell dead in finding peace, it is important that you regularly take spiritual "baths."

This consists of engaging in your spiritual practice regularly. You can also do other clearing rituals, such as with tools such as burning sage or imagining Divine Light showering down on you when you are taking a normal bath or shower. You can also imagine any energy that is less than beneficial being pulled down through your feet into the earth or imagine a Divine vacuum cleaner pulling it out of your energy field.

The biggest thing to remember when assisting the unwell or earthbound dead is that you are in charge.

You are not a victim of their antics.

Anytime you run into an earthbound spirit, you can simply say, "I release with love any energy that is not mine or is not beneficial to me." This is the quick and easy way to get rid of any non-beneficial energy, whether it is a ghost or something else. This does not necessarily help them in any way, but it does rid you of their presence.

It is really important to realize that not every bump in the night or passing shadow is a ghost! If you are constantly thinking that every out of the ordinary experience is a non-beneficial energy form of some kind, you are going to attract the very thing you are thinking about the most! Fear seems to be their food, as well as repetitive thoughts about their presence or power. Remember that what you think about grows!

Hanging out with the unwell dead is not something to do as entertainment or in hopes of harnessing their energy for some reason. They are not in connection with their highest good and in the end, the benefit you are deriving from the relationship will not end well. The only reason to connect with them is to heal them, to heal someone who is living, or to bring benefit or healing in some way to someone. If they are unwilling or unable to heal or find the light, then you need to release your contact with them, with love.

Suggested Exercises for Chapter Eleven

I never suggest you go out looking for earth-bound souls to cross over, so it is a little hard to practice this skill.

As you develop your abilities, you will occasionally run into souls who need assistance. This should serve as a reference when that happens.

Dana Robinson, Certified Teacher with the *Foundation for Shamanic Studies*https://dev.shamanism.org/fssinfo/robinsonbio.html

CHAPTER TWELVE
HEALING WITH ANCESTORS

Working with ancestors is covered in entire books and series of books, but for this book I am going to go over the basics in one chapter! I collaborated with several other healers in a series of books and journals called *The Ancestors Within**, which you can check out for a more extensive dive into working with ancestors.

Our ancestors are those who share our history, our blood, or in the case of adoption or other circumstances, they are the ones who love us despite the lack of a blood relationship.

Our original ancestors are much more ancient than those who share our bloodline. Native peoples call the Earth our Sacred Mother. Mother Earth is alive and conscious and is the one who provides us with the breath of life, the water that flows through our bodies, the food we eat and the trees, plants, stones and other life forms on this planet upon which we live.

Earth Mother is a part of the energy of the Divine. The formless energy we call God or Creator flows through the consciousness that is our Earth Mother. They are not separate from one another. Can we put a form to the wind that blows or the air we breathe? We can see the effects of the wind but we don't see the wind. We don't see the molecules or the atoms or the DNA that flows through all of life with our naked eyes but over time we have become aware of its existence.

Can we see North? Can we see East or West or South? No, we can stand facing a direction but we cannot see it.

Our ancestors' blood runs through our veins. Not only that, but they lived and died creating some aspect of who we are. We carry their DNA within us. They laughed, they cried, they loved, they grieved. Those experiences that wounded them lodged in their bodies. If they did not resolve the wounds, they passed them along for us to heal, they sometimes took those wounds to the grave and are working on the wounds on the other side, or perhaps both.

When a soul moves on to the other side, there is a place called the place of resolution. In that place, a soul gets to look over their lifetime and do a life review. They get to see how their life affected other people. They get to see how their unresolved emotions affected their choices, their experiences, and their children.

Some people who died with no regrets or unresolved issues seem to fly right on through the place of resolution, but I would venture a guess that most people have a bit of something to resolve or finish. In my former days in Christianity this was called the Judgement Seat of Christ, but now I really don't believe that we are judged by Jesus or God or anyone else. We judge ourselves. We get a chance to view our lives from beginning to end and see how our actions affected others, how our emotions or perceptions of life affected how we lived and the choices we made. If we as a living soul has judged someone on the other side, I believe a portion of their awareness stays in the place of resolution until the issue is resolved. Even if the deceased finds peace, the living need to find peace as well. As we heal ourselves, we heal our ancestors.

So, we have ancestors who are resolved and we have those who are not.

When we address an inherited issue, it is important to heal the ancestral link. It is said that our DNA goes back seven generations, so when I do a soul healing, I like to clear the bloodline up to seven generations back and seven generations forward.

I recently was in session with a client who admitted to numerous affairs while she was married and that her current love interest was technically not separated from his wife. She shared that her father had had numerous affairs, and probably her grandfather too.

Infidelity is not necessarily an inherited trait, but it can be. It normally links to an issue with intimacy. However, some people are not really programmed for monogamy, and that is okay, as long as everyone involved is aware and in agreement. The problem with infidelity is the issue of deception. For her, it related to feeling valued. When I tuned in to her father, he said he preferred that she was the one who was unfaithful, rather than the one who allowed it. His wife, my client's mother, was fully aware and did nothing. That is not to say she was okay with it; she just chose to look the other way. This seemed like disempowerment to her husband and he loathed her for it.

We can see that many powerful people are unfaithful to their spouses who decide to look the other way. Power and money are strong motivators. The problem is that when a pattern is established, it normally passes to the children.

When we heal an inherited issue, we heal everyone involved all the way back to when the pattern was established.

How do we do this?

There are many ways to shift an inherited trait.

Most of the time, I like to create a statement for the client to say to release the issue. It may go something like this:

"I lovingly release from my DNA and from my ancestral lineage the tendency to be deceptive to those I love and engage in infidelity. I release the limiting belief that I can only feel valued when deception is involved or that I need multiple partners to meet my intimacy needs. I release the trapped emotions of guilt, anger, sadness, shame, and the need to deceive. (There can be multiple issues with infidelity, not just these!! The need for adventure or risk, the need to be constantly desired by multiple people, the idea that there is something missing that I am fulfilling, the need to be found attractive or appealing, etc. etc.) I release these emotions and beliefs from everything I have experienced in this lifetime, anything I may have inherited from my ancestors, as well as any residual past life karma. I am free and lineage is free up to seven generations back and seven generations forward."

I go in to the client's energy field, find where the belief or pattern is lodged or connected and clear it out using various methods. With the help of my spirit helpers and the Divine the pattern is healed.

Once a pattern is healed, it is still up to the person who is healed to change patterns of behavior. If the activity is not changed, the pattern remains.

Our part as a healer is to allow and witness the healing. We are not really doing anything except providing a space for the nonphysical healers to do the work. Our relationship to our guides and angels or The Divine Presence is key here.

Sometimes I will use some of the tools that I describe in this book and sometimes I just provide the space and take a step back and allow The Divine to do the work. The participation and agreement of the person being healed is extremely important.

The ancestors who have healed all their wounds and ascended to the next level will most likely be there witnessing and participating in the healing. I have a place for my "next-level ancestors" on my altar. I thank them for participating and assisting in the healing.

You can't really expect assistance from an ancestor who is not healed. We may mistakenly believe that when someone passes from this life to the next, they automatically ascend and are all-benevolent and all-knowing and all-loving but this is simply not the case. All souls have free will and can choose to heal or not to heal, in physical form and in spirit.

If this is the case, is there ever an ancestor who can refuse to heal or accept a healing for a pattern we are addressing? Yes! I have had this happen. There is really nothing we can do to make someone heal if they don't want to. However, we can cut the cord that attaches us to a particular pattern so we are no longer affected and our children are not affected. (Cord cutting will be discussed later.)

What if we heal an ancestral pattern and our child is an adult and is engaging in an inherited pattern? We heal the DNA and the bloodline, and know that the adult child has free will and is free to accept the healing or not. Remember, we have three aspects to our soul. We have the part of our soul that is new for this lifetime. We have the part we inherit through our bloodline, and we have the part we bring with us from other lifetimes and dimensions.

I have attempted to go in through the back door of ancestral patterns and heal issues without the consent of the person who is suffering. I was successful in healing the ancestral link but the person still had the issue until she was willing to face it herself and choose to shift the pattern for her current lifetime.

Many parents come to me hoping to heal their dysfunctional children, from toddlers to adults. Whether a child is an infant or middle aged, we cannot cross free will. If verbal consent is not given, it is possible to gain consent from their soul, but this is not always given. It is possible that their soul chose to experience a particular pattern for their own evolution or for some other purpose. If we ask the soul and the soul refuses, we have to honor their choice.

Once, I was meditating before a client called for her healing session and my mother on the other side showed up. She seemed angry and was coming at me strong! I was so surprised because I thought we had resolved all of our issues. I had gone back and healed a lot of the unexpressed anger my mother felt inside that I also felt while in the womb and growing up. In my vision there was a glass shield which deflected her anger towards me.

As a child my mother was always involved in spiritual service. I judged her, because I felt she never had time for us, her actual children. She would give away things that I thought she should have kept. She invited some of my aunts and cousins to live with us at various times, while they were going through difficulties. Everyone in the family loved her. My cousins often commented on the impact she had had in their lives. Although I enjoyed the company of those who came to stay with us for periods of time, I always felt that my mother was a loving presence to everyone else except to me. I once heard her say to one of my cousins: "you are like a daughter to me." I remember feeling very conflicted about this statement, since my relationship with my mother was complicated. I interpreted this to mean she wished my cousin was her daughter instead of my sister or myself.

I was recently watching a documentary about the well-known comedian Robin Williams. In an interview with his son, he remarked that he sometimes resented the gift his father was to the world because that meant he was very much an absentee father. I realized that this was also true for me. My mother was a gift to many but very much absent for me in a heart connection with her.

Whether or not my mother actually felt that her children were a distraction from her purpose in life, I cannot say, since she denies it, even from the other side. However, in story of my interaction with my deceased mother while meditating, I was getting a distinct feeling that she believed that her real blood daughters were keeping her from fulfilling her mission in life. In her eyes, serving Jesus was her reason for being here. At her death, the pastor asked people to come up and speak and tell what a blessing my mother was to them. Although I realized that many people loved her and she gave herself in service to God in a real and tangible way, I resented that I never really felt valued by her.

I will admit that this judgement I had of her came back to haunt me. In my own born-again Christian experience, I often prioritized my service to the church over my daughter. I did not recognize it until after I had departed that belief system, but hindsight is often a cruel teacher.

Was this the fault of the belief system or a character flaw in my ancestry? Service to others and denial of personal needs was often very much encouraged, but not everyone who went to church neglected their own children's needs in service to the church.

In my case, the issue probably went further back than my mother.

My mother's mother had eleven children. They were poor and I am sure her whole life revolved around caring for all of these children. In those days I am sure birth control was not easily accessible, if it was even available, especially to poor people, and I can imagine she didn't really want all of those children. I realized that my perception of my mother's unexpressed anger that her children were keeping her from following her path in life may have also been true of her own mother.

I cleared the inherited pattern or limiting belief that "children are a distraction from fulfilling my real purpose in life or experiencing joy" seven generations back. Who knows what other stories my great-grandmothers may have to tell?

Interestingly enough, my client called just as I finished my session with my mother and her issues were with her mother. The issues between her and her mother were almost identical to the issues I had just been working on with my own mother.

Isn't it funny how that works?

My mother made herself vulnerable from the other side and addressed these issues with me before my session with my client so I could assist my client in healing her issues with her mother.

Thanks mom.

Ancestral healing is not just about healing the unaddressed wounds of our ancestors and removing them from the bloodline.

Our ancestors can be assets in our healing work! They will often come in to assist us in healing others.

Just as we have inherited wounds from them, we have also inherited gifts!

Now that I am much older and my mother has been gone for many years, I recognize myself behaving in ways that used to infuriate me about her! However, I acknowledge the strength of character she had and the compulsion to assist people no matter what the cost to her personal convenience. The day before she passed of cancer, she was driving elderly ladies around paying their bills, getting their medicine, and balancing their checkbooks. She was clearly suffering but she set her own pain aside to be of service to others.

It is important to recognize that our ancestors go back much further than the ones we knew in life or have been told about or learned about through sitting around chatting with family.

They like helping us when we embark upon a path of healing. They like hanging out and watching us no matter what path we choose in life!

In some cultures, there is not much interaction with angels, guides, The Divine, or even power animals. All of the assistance is believed to come from the ancestors.

In life my dad was a strong Christian. His brother was a minister and his sister was married to one! Their children all entered "the ministry." In my very young days, before dad took ill, he pastored a small church in rural Virginia.

After he gave up the ministry, he and my mother remained extremely active in the local Assembly of God church.

At first, I was hesitant to call upon my parents for assistance in my healing work, because their belief system was a far cry from the way I currently follow my spiritual path. I have been continually surprised when they show up anyway! Even one of my uncles who pastored a church for over fifty years occasionally shows up!

Our good and loving ancestral helping spirits are there to assist us as we live our lives. We can ask them for simple things, like finding lost keys or we can ask them to assist us in the big stuff.

There are so many aspects to ancestral healing, and this is such a short description of how to heal with and for our ancestors. Please refer to other sources, including *The Ancestors Within** series of books to continue your education.

Some Exercises for Chapter Twelve

Using some of your skills you have been working on in previous chapters, do a meditation or shamanic journey and connect with some of your ancestors. Ask them if they have any wisdom to share or perhaps if they can let you in on any family secrets or patterns that need to be shifted.

If you can look at your ancestry and identify some inherited traits, work on releasing them from the family tree, using the suggested statements or create one of your own.

If you receive information from an ancestor, it is my practice to always ask them to tell you something you can verify to solidify that you did indeed receive information from them. This boosts your own confidence in the information received and also is a safeguard to you to prevent you from receiving inaccurate information. If you have no way of verifying some of the information, then ask them to send confirmation a different way.

In the aforementioned story about my mother, the confirmation was immediate. My client wanted to address nearly identical issues with her mother.

Be sure to write down any information you receive when connecting with the ancestors. This shows them that you value their interaction with them and inspires them to return.

Always bless and acknowledge your ancestors. You may decide to create a sacred place, like an altar or other place of honor, where you acknowledge your ancestors and thank them for their contribution into the life you now enjoy. Despite any lack of character issues, your ancestors are the reason you are here! You can acknowledge the ancestors you know with items that remind you of them. You can also acknowledge your heritage with items from the place where you are from. It is okay to insist that any unhealed ancestors not interact with your or interfere in your life, even while acknowledging the gift of life they gave you.

Think about creating a place of honor for your ancestors. Light a candle and thank them for their gifts to you. Periodically address them and welcome them to be a part of your life. I like to offer them gifts on occasion.

You can read more about creating an ancestor altar here.

https://www.whispersofjoy.net/single-post/honoring-our-ancestors

The Ancestors Within, (series of 4 books available on Amazon by Amy Gillespie and other authors including Joy Andreasen by Brave Healer Productions

PART III

OTHER HEALING TOOLS AND MODALITIES

CHAPTER THIRTEEN

CREATING OUR OWN PERSONAL MEDICINE BAG

We all are unique souls with experience and connection to our own unique set of healing guides and tools. Each of us is in the process of creating our own personal "medicine bag" of healing tools. Depending on our heritage, our past lives, our current lives, our time in between earth lifetimes, and our own healing team we will each have our own methods that work really well for us or maybe not work at all.

You don't have to have a desire to assist others in healing to find value in continuing on in this section. Self-healing and a desire to enhance your own spiritual journey is all that is necessary! This information is truly valuable when embarking upon a path of self-discovery!

When I speak of my "medicine bag," I am not talking about an actual bag containing my various tools, such as feathers, crystals, sage or candles that I use for healing, although I do have one of those. I am actually referring to the various healing modalities I have come across during my years of spiritual exploration.

As I describe some various "tools" I have either learned or discovered on my own, I place each one into my own personal spiritual toolbox. Depending on the situation, I may pull out a different tool. In this section, I will describe some of the tools in my toolbox that I haven't covered yet.

Some of the healing modalities I will share in this section already have been copyrighted, registered, and trademarked, and already have books written about them and training classes are offered by

143

their creators. I will give credit to the creators and I will not try to explain how to do them in any detail. I will offer you links to the websites or books that describe them. I don't want to infringe on any copyright laws. My intention is to give credit to the teachers and creators of healing methods that I love or that work for me.

All of us who are on a spiritual journey to total wellness are creating our path as we go along. I often combine different healing methods in my sessions with clients. I don't hold a certification in any of these methods other than Reiki because when you get that certificate, you often have to agree to do the healing sessions exactly the way they are taught by their creators. I don't fault the creators of these healing methods for this. I just don't work that way.

If you feel a draw to be a healer, you will have to decide for yourself what modality you want to explore and use in your own practice. You may decide to train with a particular teacher or abide to a specific modality, or you may want to use a variety of tools to bring about a shift for those who come to you.

Whether you are looking for a healer, or you want to be one, I hope that you will educate yourself on a variety of tools and find the ones that feel good to you.

Most of the tools I describe can be used for personal self-healing or to assist others in aligning with their own sense of wellness.

Don't consider yourself a master after reading this book or any other!

No certificate of mastery makes you a master!

Read these next chapters carefully and do the suggested exercises to see if they resonate with you. If they do and you are able to find benefit to the particular tool, you may want to explore any further education recommended and practice with the tools for a while before moving on.

My hope is that these tools for wellness benefit you personally and that you refer back to the material frequently for reference.

CHAPTER FOURTEEN
HEALING WITH LIGHT, SOUND, AND MOVEMENT

Healing With Light

One of the first methods I used in self-healing I actually taught myself, or I should say, was given to me by my guides, although I would not have admitted to having guides at the time. I was still very much engaged in my born-again Christian beliefs, and therefore the only healer was Jesus or the Holy Spirit. So technically it is possible this healing method was given to me by Jesus.

In my late twenties I injured my back working for the Post Office, and every so often, I would have an episode of disc injuries. Subsequent MRIs would reveal disc abnormalities and subsequent arthritis which, according to my chiropractor, should have created significant continuous pain.

Early on, I would frequently find myself in the bed for days, only rolling out of bed to crawl to the bathroom on my hands and knees. During those hours, I would meditate, read a variety of spiritual books and journal about my life.

One day I was laying in the bed and I was instructed to visualize tiny balls of light and send them into my back. Sometimes they just looked like white light, and I would see them going into my back and reforming my nerves and discs. Sometimes they looked like cotton candy, and I would observe them going in between the discs that were rubbing against one another and forming a sort of cushion in between the discs. Some days they appeared as tiny little *Pac-Mans** eating away at the pain.

In other chapters I discuss the correlation between emotions, beliefs and physical pain, and how certain body parts often present with physical complaints due to stress related to the chakra where the pain is located. Here I let you in on the secret of how I nearly completely eliminated the pain!

I began to notice that the pain in my back began to heal more quickly. I went from two weeks in bed to one week, to a few days, to a day, and now, I only occasionally feel a twinge in my back which I am usually able to heal in hours, and sometimes minutes!

I have healed the emotional triggers which created the pain in the first place. I have eliminated the toxic relationship which created ongoing stress about money and survival. And now I use light and visualization to eliminate pain!

My last MRI over ten years ago revealed that nothing had really changed physically. My doctors seemed amazed that I am rarely in pain.

More recently, a knee injury debilitated me for quite a bit longer. Truthfully, I had forgotten about the little Pac-Mans and the light visualization! However, I did eventually remember, and despite my doctor telling me I would need frequent injections and possible eventual surgery, most of the time I forget about the injury completely.

Now I have an almost daily ritual of bathing myself with Light.

The Benevolent Helpers use Divine Light and Sound to remind our souls and our physical bodies of who we are! By connecting to the Light of our Souls and the Light Beings, whatever you want to call them, you can shift your physical, mental, emotional and spiritual bodies to a more highly evolved version of yourself, and you can use this technique on others as well!

By using your skills at visualization, and the technique of shamanic journeying which you should have been practicing from the previous section, you can create a lovely healing experience where you go regularly and receive Divine Light injections or showers or however you want to experience it!

In the book *Healing Yourself with Light** by LaUna Huffines, there are a number of meditations where you create a healing temple complete with various rooms of healing with light, color, sound, and stillness. You connect with the light of your soul and what she calls your Solar Angel. I won't repeat what she has written, but in your visualizations or spiritual journeys, simply imagine taking a shower from the Light of the Creator which showers down on you from Above.

You can do what I did and create forms that cushion your bones or eat away at the pain.

You can imagine all of the cells in your body being infused with various colors of Divine Light.

Exercise: Healing with Light

Get into a meditative state. Relax your body and close your eyes.

Sit for a moment in silence.

Imagine the light of your soul inside of your body.

Feel the love coming from your soul.

Send a beam of light from the light of your soul down into Mother Earth and connect with the soul of the Earth Mother. Bring your awareness back up into your soul's light, while remaining connected to her.

Now send a beam of light from your soul up into the heavens, where the Creator resides. Feel the Light of the Creator joining with the light of your soul.

Imagine that all of the cells in your body are being infused with the Light of the Creator. You may see a variety of colors or you may only see white. Every color has its own healing vibration, so allow whatever colors show up to do their work. You may decide to go through all of the varieties of colors one by one, allowing that particular color to do its work, or you may intuitively be led to a particular color or sequence of colors.

There are no "bad" colors.

You can be creative and visualize the color coming into your body in a variety of ways. Allow your Guides and your higher self to lead the way.

Stay with this experience as long as you feel led.

Healing With Sound and/or Movement

All of us have within us the sound of our souls. We could call it our soul's song.

If we get really still and listen, we can hear it!

It could be just one note, or it could be a full-length song.

We can only hear the song of our soul by getting quiet and listening.

If you are musical, you could perhaps listen for your song, and sing it, or perhaps play it on an instrument.

In my former life as a tongue-talking, jig-dancing Pentecostal, we called this *Dancing or Singing in the Spirit.* However, many belief systems have some sort of song, music, or movement ritual that is inherent in the spiritual experience. Native people drum, rattle, and dance. Buddhists chant.

Within our soul, we know that song and movement heal. If you are in any way immobile but still have the ability to think or visualize, you can imagine that you are moving!

148

One of my favorite shamanic journeys I take regularly is when I imagine going to this beautiful meadow and inviting all my loving ancestors, guides, angels and allies to join me for a dance! I either create the music in my imagination or I put on happy music and imagine dancing with them! Sometimes I listen quietly for the song of my soul and allow a spontaneous song to emerge from within me. It may or may not have words. As I mentioned before, in my former belief system, we had what we called *Praying in Tongues.* The New Age community has a similar experience called *Light Language.* (Spoiler alert: it is the same thing – different name.) All you have to do is get still. Listen for a song or a note to come up from inside your soul and then open your mouth and make a sound or series of sounds or words. The words may or may not be in your native language or any language you recognize. The words are not important. It is the sound that heals.

Healing With Sound Exercise

If you are going to be moving around, make sure you set a space that is clear of obstructions or hazards.

Close your eyes and stand or sit in silence.

Listen to your soul for a moment and see if you can hear the song of your soul.

You can hum a note that you hear or a series of sounds that create a song. If words come, then sing the words.

You can use instruments like drums, rattles, crystal bowls, bells, or you can put on some music that inspires you, but eventually you want to create the sound yourself. If you are not vocal, you can hum the sound inside of your head.

If you are able, allow the sound of your soul to inspire movement of some sort.

Using Sound and Light to Bring Healing to Others

Before you try to use this technique on others, you should have had regular sessions of sending light and sound into your own experience. Experiment with both light and sound. Create regular sessions of sound or light meditations, where you are infusing your cells with Divine Light and Divine Sound. Know the song of your soul.

When using this technique on others, begin by connecting with the light of your soul. Send a beam of light down to connect with the Earth Mother, and then a beam of light up to the Creator.

Now you are going to imagine creating another beam of light down through the crown chakra of your recipient. From the Creator, you will be given the color that is most beneficial for your recipient. If in doubt, pink is always my favorite. Pink is the color of compassion and higher love. I often send beams of pink light to my family members, friends and clients and always qualify that the light is for the highest good with the agreement of their soul and free will. However, you may feel led to use a different color.

Give the recipient a full "bath" or "shower" of light, color and sound.

Perhaps you may want to visualize them in the middle of a circle of your Angels and Guides. Everyone is dancing around them and singing a song into their energy field.

There is no right or wrong way to heal with light and sound as long as you have the recipient's highest good as the intended outcome!

Suggested Exercises for Chapter Fourteen

Take some time in doing the healing exercises with light, sound, and movement. It is important that you not judge yourself for the sounds or movements that present themselves spontaneously into your experience.

If you decide to do this for others, you may find yourself dancing around your recipient, singing the song of your soul, perhaps drumming or using other instruments of sound. Watch how the frequency of your sessions change when you incorporate light, sound and movement into the healing experience.

You may choose to work exclusively with this method! I really like it and find it to be extremely effective.

*www.Pacman.com

*Healing Yourself with Light – How to Connect with the Angelic Healers by LaUna Huffines, copyright 1995 by H J Kramer in a joint venture with New World Library

CHAPTER FIFTEEN
HEALING WITH A PENDULUM

Before I discovered the skill of using a pendulum to shift energy, I only knew it as a divination tool, and not a very good one, actually. I had a pendulum. It worked sometimes, but not enough to be a regular tool for divination.

Most people use a pendulum to get yes and no answers. There are various charts you can find online in which you are using it kind of like a Ouija board. Each letter or number is on a particular place on the chart, and the pendulum swings toward letters which spell out words and phrases. I have never used it this way, but have spoken to people who have good success.

The theory of working with a pendulum to heal or to shift energy is that a pendulum is a tool that we can gain mastery of to use as an extension of our own energy and the energy of our healing team.

In order to gain mastery of the use of a pendulum, you must familiarize yourself with its various uses. You must take some time to learn how energy is shifted in yourself and in the astral realms where change happens first before it occurs in our physical experience.

I am not including a chart in this book, but if you are familiar with the face of a clock, you have a chart. Basically, to use a pendulum as a tool for healing or shifting energy, you only need to know a couple of things.

SACRED PATH TO WELLNESS

Your pendulum is an extension of your own healing energy. When you hold the pendulum in your hand, and you set an intention, the pendulum naturally begins to swing.

In various belief systems, it is commonly known that when you want to bring something in to your experience, you incorporate the phases of the moon and the directions. The time of the waxing moon, or the roughly two weeks before a full moon, is good for manifesting or bringing things in to your life, and the waning moon, or the time after the full moon and before the new moon, is a good time for releasing non-beneficial aspects of your life. In the same way, if you think about the face of a clock, the direction of clockwise is good for bringing in to your life, and counter-clockwise is good for releasing.

The face of a clock can be used along with the pendulum to release and manifest and to find out what percentage you are aligned with your highest good.

So, for example, if you hold your pendulum between your forefinger and your thumb, and allow the chain to be only a couple of inches long before reaching the crystal or whatever is at the end of it, and you say, "I now align my energy with my highest good," the pendulum should begin to circle clockwise.

You can be as general or as specific as you like, but, as I have previously mentioned, make sure your statements do not interfere with someone's free will or cause harm in any way.

After the pendulum has done its work, you can ask if the work is complete, and, if not, what percentage is it complete. Percentages work along with the numbers on a clock. Twelve o'clock is zero percent, three o'clock is one hundred percent. If the pendulum swings toward the 1, you are about thirty three percent aligned with your highest good. If the pendulum swings between 9 and 12, then you are in a negative percentage of being aligned with your highest good and have some work to do! I very rarely have the pendulum

153

swing between 3 and 9 when asking this particular question. The intention is to see improvement. You may not get to 100 percent right away, but you may. You may get to 100 percent for today but tomorrow is another story. Every day we are responsible for our energy field and for aligning ourselves to our highest good.

Your intention and your relationship to your Guides is what makes the pendulum work. My Guides told me that the pendulum uses the elements of air and earth to bring about changes. Any tool or ritual needs to bring what is done in the astral realms into the realm of Earth in order to bring about changes in someone's life. We can do positive affirmations and mantras all day long, but if we don't bring them into our physical body experience, nothing will change. In other words, if I want to lose twenty pounds, and every day I am saying, "I am perfectly aligned with my ideal weight for my body" and we say it a hundred times a day, but continue to eat ice cream and potato chips, nothing is going to change. Some action on our part is needed. The pendulum brings what we are intending and saying in the astral realms into our physical reality and assists us in making the needed changes in our actions.

We can use the pendulum along with other healing modalities by using it to remove unwanted energy that lodges in one of our four energy bodies, which we covered previously.

What energy gets stuck in our body?

There are a number of possibilities. I will name a few here, but cover them more in depth later.

We as souls are multidimensional beings. We are flesh and blood, yes, but we are also every thought we have ever had, every emotion we have felt, every belief we have ever formulated based on the thoughts and emotions, not only we have had in this lifetime, but every other experience we have had as a soul, and many times the unresolved emotions and beliefs of our ancestors.

Sometimes energy gets stuck in our bodies which is not even ours! It takes intuition and trust in what the Guides tell you in order to know whether someone's headache is a result of allergies, of sinus pressure, of a tumor, of an ancestral link, an attachment from some energy that should not be there, or any number of possibilities. I recently had a client who came in with a headache. I felt it energetically which she confirmed. Her ancestors came through and told me that it was partially because she had not consumed her normal amount of caffeine that day and partially the poor air quality at work. They told her to drink a little caffeine and try to go outside once in a while and get some fresh air! It is not completely necessary when working on someone's headache to know exactly where the source of the pain is, but it is certainly helpful. After she confirmed the details, I used the pendulum to reduce her headache pain. The pendulum began to swing counter-clockwise and I said the affirmation that the pain from lack of caffeine and poor air quality was being released from her body along with any other non-beneficial factors. After the pendulum stopped circling, I then said the affirmation that her physical body was aligning with her highest good. She confirmed relief of the headache!

Many times, when I am doing sessions with clients, I will be given information about stuck beliefs and emotions which need removed from the client. I normally give the client an affirmation to say while I am pulling the undesired energetic imbalance out of the client. I find it to be a valuable tool when the client is aware and engaged with the healing.

In the best possible scenario, I am given the core belief or emotion which is at the foundation of the problem. If you are able to detect the core belief, the other beliefs seem to easily be neutralized. However, Spirit doesn't always work this way. Healing is a process. Sometimes it can be immediate and sometimes it is incremental. I find that many times our conscious awareness cannot handle a whole reprogramming in one session. Most of our beliefs were formulated at a young age, or even outside of the perimeter of this particular lifetime, and although we may have forgotten a good bit of our experiences from childhood, the beliefs remain in our subconscious. This subconscious is on autopilot, bringing experiences into our lives over and over to reinforce a belief or trauma.

It took me years to reprogram my beliefs after I began to disassociate with the religious views I had been born into. There was much fear and misguided belief which had directed and controlled me for my entire life. I could not immediately discard them and reinvent myself. My identity was entirely wrapped up in what I believed about God and the world. When that was taken away, I did not know who I was without those beliefs. This cannot happen in the blink of an eye! If I go my whole life believing I am one thing only to find out that what I believed was flawed, I cannot immediately jump into a completely different version of myself. Give yourself and your clients time to acclimate to this new version of themselves!

If you are using a pendulum to do a healing, this is how I recommend you incorporate it into your healing work. Before you start, you can ask the pendulum if you are energetically aligned with your client, if they are open to a healing, and ask that any obstacles or resistance be neutralized.

1. Connect with your Source of Power. This process was described previously using various methods, but it is vitally important to connect with Source or your Guides before doing a healing.

2. Ask permission of the recipient of the healing.

3. While connected to your Source, connect with your recipient's energy field by taking your awareness into their body, either

through their crown chakra or sometimes I go in through the heart chakra.

4. Begin to allow your intuition to do a scan of the person's energy field and identify an area to be worked on. This could relate to a physical concern, or a mental, emotional, or spiritual concern. (Scanning a person's energy field was described in Chapter 5).

5. If you "see" an area of concern, you can approach it a number of ways. You can describe to the recipient what you are sensing and see if they can agree with your assessment. If so, if this is something to be released, such as anger lodged in the liver, for example, you can do further scanning to see if you can identify where the source of the anger is. For example, if the recipient holds anger against their father, you can have the recipient declare: "I now release anger toward my father" as you focus on allowing the pendulum to swing counter-clockwise and remove the intrusion of the anger in to the liver. Most times it is a bit more complicated than just that, but this is a simple example for now. We will chat a bit about emotions and beliefs in the next chapter.

6. After the pendulum stops rotating counter-clockwise, allow it to stop. You are then going to replace where the anger was with the energy of the Divine and the energy of the recipient's highest good. The pendulum should then swing clockwise as you say either aloud or inside yourself that you are aligning the recipient with their highest good and with the energy of the Divine.

7. You can now ask your pendulum what percentage the recipient is aligned to their highest good. The ultimate goal is 100 percent, of course. If you receive an answer that is less than that, you can keep going until you reach 100 percent, or stop if you feel the recipient is resistant to their highest good. If you have been practicing and honing your psychic muscles, you will be able to feel the resistance.

If you want to just practice a bit, begin by saying an intention, such as "I neutralize any blocks to my highest good," (counter-clockwise) or "I align my energy to my highest good" (clockwise). These are wonderful general statements that always work.

Remember that in the same way you need to bathe your physical body regularly, you need to cleanse your energy body and your space regularly. This is not a one time, fix all, solution. You may register at 100 percent today and 10 percent tomorrow. Our emotions, beliefs, thoughts and life circumstances will shift our energy regularly.

If you find you are frequently revisiting issues either in yourself or your clients regularly, remember that healing is a process. Just like the layers of an onion, if there is a dark spot in the outer layer of the onion, there is a good chance it shows up in the underneath layers, but you can't see it until you peel off or cut out the spot on the top layer. There will be progress, and setbacks. There will be healing and sometimes there will be times when you feel like you just can't get past a certain issue. Something is holding it there. Sometimes as healers we are able to get to the heart of issue immediately and sometimes it takes time.

The use of a pendulum is a valuable tool in shifting energy that certainly can be accomplished in a variety of ways.

Shifting energy is not just about healing a human being. You can use it to work on animals, plants, the earth, your bank account, and countless other energy intrusions that come up in our life on Earth.

Once I was doing an event in an area of West Virginia where the internet was spotty. My assistant was having trouble taking credit card payments and had to interrupt me while I was doing readings to try to fix the problem. I took my pendulum and circled it above my phone where I take payments. I said, "I align my phone and my credit card app with the energy of perfect connection to the internet. I align this area with perfect internet connection." Within a few seconds the credit card app began working and we experienced no more issues that day. I did the same thing for a client whose internet at her home was spotty. The rest of the day her internet worked perfectly, even while using multiple devices. Once again, this is not a one-time-fix-all solution. You may need to address the problem or find yourself having to pendulum your internet every day.

It is not always a good idea to pendulum your electronic items such as laptops, phones or connectivity issues. I find when my Guides want me to take a break or focus on something else, my computer will begin to act up. Remember that everything is connected. Sometimes you may just need to disconnect. However, I also find that sometimes there will be resistance on the part of the client which will affect the connection if I am doing a session by Zoom or some other video platform. I have often been able to improve the connection by neutralizing the resistance to the work that is being done, and I do this with my pendulum.

When using any tool for healing or divination, you must understand that you are in charge! Your intentions and your statements are creating the shift and empowering your pendulum or other tool. The tool is an extension of your energy field. You may want to imagine that your hands are extending out and that the power is flowing into the pendulum. You are in charge in what you are commanding or requesting of your pendulum or your healing session. It is not that you are claiming that the power rests in your own ability. It rests in your connection to your Source and your understanding that your connection is more powerful than anything that may oppose it. The only thing that can interfere with the power of healing or shifting energy using the pendulum or any other tool is your own lack of awareness and understanding of your connection with the Guides, your confidence in your tool or your ability to use the tool, and the client's or recipient's free will or their own blocks.

One of the most common problems I see when teaching students is their own limiting beliefs about their own power or abilities and in the belief that the dark is more powerful than the light.

Fear is almost idolized in these modern days. People flock to horror movies, crazy amusement park rides, stories of ghosts that attack and injure people, demons, and tragedies. Fear is the food of the dark. It is important to realize that you are not victim to the dark.

I once had a young person who lived in a low-income apartment in the town where I live call me and ask me to come rid his apartment of a ghost. I told him I could clear the apartment remotely; I did not need to come in person. When I tuned in, I realized that drugs were a frequent occurrence at the apartment and within the surrounding apartments. The energies he felt were indeed welcome there because they were attached to the drug use. There was also frequent arguing and discord. I shared with him what I saw and he insisted this activity was not him but the apartments around him. Using the pendulum, from the comfort of my home, I rid his apartment of the dark energy and set a boundary around his apartment so the "ghost" could not enter. I told him if I did this and he was lying to me, that he would be unable to participate in any drug use in his apartment, because the spirits were not allowed in the apartment. I told him if he still experienced activity after I did the remote session to call me back and I would come in person. I never heard back from him.

I have also cleared and blessed land using the pendulum, cleared water and food, cleared medicine of any non-compatible or non-beneficial ingredients, and more! If you can think of anything you would like to remove or neutralize, you can use the pendulum. If there is anything you want to align yourself with, you can use the pendulum.

One of the best aspects of the pendulum is that you can carry it around with you practically anywhere. My daughter is a CNA and her specialty is the elderly. As you can imagine, she frequently finds herself in places where the deceased have not crossed or there are unresolved emotions stuck in the buildings or rooms. Obviously, she cannot carry sage around with her or other more well-known and popular means of clearing space, but the pendulum works just as well. When she was working in a particular facility, she would frequently run into energy and would pull out her trusty pendulum and help any way she could and only if she was allowed. She did forbid them from following her home or interfering with her work. Back when I worked full-time, I didn't necessarily want to pull my pendulum out in front of everyone, but I would go into the bathroom, enter a stall and pull out the pendulum to clear space or direct energy.

- WHAT CAN'T YOU DO?

1. You can't fix someone who does not want to be fixed.

2. You can't interfere with someone's soul purpose. Fate is what a soul has decided beforehand to experience in this lifetime. You can't change that. Destiny is a given potential based upon an intended projectory of events. You can change that.

3. Remember that sometimes things just happen. No matter what you do some things just don't change. You have to be willing to give up an attachment to a particular outcome.

Remember that the pendulum is not a magic ball! Your intentions, your connection with Source energy, and your skills are developed over time. As you practice with the pendulum, you will begin to be led by Spirit in uses for it.

Suggested Exercises for Chapter Fifteen

I suggest having more than one pendulum. Remember that your tools are extensions of your energy field, but they also have their own form of consciousness. Connect with the consciousness of any tool you use. Ask it to work with you. Honor your tools. Let them rest on occasion.

Play with your pendulum and see what all you can do with it. A lot of alternative healing techniques that require close physical contact can be eliminated by using the pendulum to do the work.

Remember that the pendulum is a tool. Make sure you are connected to the energy of Divine Love or the highest available Benevolent Helpers before using it. Also make sure you are properly hydrated as it will not work well otherwise.

*I honed my understanding of the pendulum and what is commonly called Dowsing by Raymon Grace

www.raymongracefoundation.org

CHAPTER SIXTEEN

THE POWER OF EMOTIONS

In the world of healing, beliefs and emotions are extremely important in getting to the heart of a lot of issues.

I already chatted with you about my love for Louise Hay's book, *You Can Heal Your Life*, and how reading this book changed my life and introduced me to the idea that my thoughts and emotions were directly linked to specific physical maladies.

Recently I was chatting with my daughter about her recurring heartburn. I reminded her that heartburn often has to do with unexpressed anger. She mused that she had not really had much difficulty since she had eliminated a specific relationship from her life. I mused that my anger toward the same person manifested as urinary tract infections. My immediate message from the Guides was that similar emotions manifest in a particular part of the body based on where the relationship attached to the body. Her relationship "cord" to this person was in or near the heart chakra and mine was in or near the sacral chakra. This may give you a hint as to the identity of this person, but suffice it to say that since we both eliminated our relationship to this person, our symptoms have disappeared.

The important point here is that when we are in relationship with people, we create energetic cords that attach us to them. They attach near or around the chakra that most defines the relationship. We may have multiple cords based on the complexity of relationships. The area of difficulty in the body is related to the area of difficulty in the relationship. The emotions we feel but do not release in a healthy manner are the ones that become lodged in our body near the chakra that defines the challenging part of the relationship.

Recently in a session with a client I found the emotion of guilt that was lodged in her body from her mother and her father, however, the guilt was lodged in different areas of the body. The guilt had a cord attached to her father in her heart chakra and the same emotion of guilt had a cord related to her mother in her sacral chakra. The guilt was not necessarily originating from her. I felt the guilt had originated from each of her parents and even possibly grandparents and was being transmitted to her from them. Yes! Sometimes the emotions are passed down through the bloodline but we find ourselves suffering because of these unresolved emotions.

This method associates various body parts with the chakra they are closest in proximity to. Most of the time just looking at the affected body part and noticing which chakra it is closest to will give you a hint of certain blocks or emotions which may be interfering with health and even may give you a hint of the relationship or challenge in the person's life that is creating the energetic intrusion.

I am not going to include a list of all the possible emotions here in this book, but you can easily find multiple charts just by doing a simple internet search.

If you are trying to find what emotions are linked to a client's issues, and your own intuitive sense is not developed enough yet or you are not getting a hit, I recommend you obtain a chart of some kind.

If you have a chart, you can use your pendulum or other muscle testing techniques I don't elaborate on in this book to discover what the trapped or unresolved emotion is and where it is trapped in the energy field.

When you discover a trapped emotion in a person's energy field, sometimes it is helpful to discover a little more about why it is trapped there, how long it has been there, and why it got stuck. Although this is not completely necessary, sometimes when you just eliminate or neutralize a stuck emotion and don't find out why or how it got stuck, you will find the emotion getting stuck again at some point in the future.

Remember that a stuck emotion could have multiple sources of entry. We previously learned that we are made up of the part we inherit from our ancestors, the part we brought in from other lifetimes or dimensions, and the part we create in this lifetime.

If you are skilled intuitively, you can sense the emotion and the source. You may sense where it is trapped in the body, and get a sense of where it originated. Because I am skilled at connecting with the deceased, I will often see a particular ancestor and feel his or her emotions and sense that the emotion was passed down through the DNA. Sometimes I will see an image that could not have occurred in this lifetime and I will have to do some digging to see if I am seeing a previous lifetime, an ancestor, or even a metaphor to something that happened in this lifetime. Normally I will share with my client what I am seeing, and we will follow it to see where it leads.

There are a number of ways to eliminate a trapped emotion.

In my previous example of my daughter and I having the same emotion trapped in our body in different locations based on a particular relationship, when we eliminated the source of our anger, we eliminated the health difficulty. Sometimes it is that simple! There is no healing session necessary! Just eliminate the source of the difficult emotion! You can have a hundred healing sessions, but if the source of the trapped emotion is not eliminated, your healing success will be short lived!

But if you are working on healing or eliminating a trapped emotion from the body with a source that perhaps is ancient or undefined, there are multiple ways to remove, clear, resolve, or neutralize it.

• You can use your pendulum to remove it while keeping your client aware of what you are doing. It is important that your client be aware and in agreement to the healing work. Although you are allowing your Guides to remove the emotional intrusion, you are sharing with your client what you are seeing or sensing or doing.

• You may find it beneficial to give the client a statement or affirmation to repeat while doing the work.

For example, let's say the client has unresolved anger toward a lover who rejected her. (This is fairly common so it makes a good example.) While scanning her energy field, you notice the anger lodged in her sacral and heart chakra. (Common locations for the anger lodged based on rejection from a lover.) She agrees that she is angry. However, you feel the anger goes further back than just this particular relationship. (It probably does.) You can choose to go further back and expose every time she was jilted or rejected or you can give her a statement to say while you are pulling the anger out.

Here would be an example of a statement to have your client say while releasing the anger:

"With the help of Divine Love, I release all anger from every romantic rejection in this lifetime, in any other lifetime, and any anger I may have inherited from my ancestors, up to seven generations back, and I also release it seven generations forward. I release any other emotions and beliefs lodged in my body empowering this emotion to remain stuck. I clear it from all time, space and dimensions. I forgive all who have made me angry, including myself. I declare that I am free."

It is not completely necessary to have the client say the statement out loud, but I find it helps in having your client a conscious partner to the healing. Saying the words seems to have the effect of dislodging the stuck emotion and getting it released.

Remember also the emotion can be lodged in any one of the four energy fields we previously discussed. You can add to the statement that is being removed from all four energy fields, or the one you feel it is lodged in.

If you are using the pendulum, remember to make sure your pendulum is rotating counter-clockwise while you are visualizing removing the intrusion from the client's energy field.

• You may "see" the intrusion in various ways. Imagine being in his or her energy field and scooping out the anger, or removing it from their field. You are completely being led by your Guides when doing this work. The Guides will use different means to remove the emotion from the energy field.

• If you are connected to the energy of the Divine Source, the Creator of All That Is when doing this work, you are simply a witness as you watch what appears to me as Light Energy dissolving or eliminating the trapped emotion. This may be discerned in various ways. You may see the Light dissolve the emotion. You may feel it or sense it in some other way.

• You can visualize yourself in that person's energy field removing it.

• You can use Reiki or other healing modalities to remove it.

• You can use the feather technique or crystals or stones.

• You can channel your Guides or the Divine Source Energy and just watch them do it.

• Here I would like to insert a method using a magnet to remove difficult or unresolved emotions. The book that describes this method is called *The Emotion Code* and is written by Dr. Bradley Nelson. * In this method, you use a magnet to pull the emotions out of the body. You would do this by being in the person's

167

presence, or by using a surrogate to act as the channel for the healing to occur. I find this method extremely effective and highly recommend it. I am not going to elaborate a lot here, since Dr Nelson has done an excellent job in his own published works.

Whatever method you use, there are a couple of important things to remember.

You can't be in completely waking alert consciousness to do this work. Most healers enter into a bit of an altered state of consciousness while doing healing work. This state is commonly called Alpha state, and it is when your brain waves slow down to a daydream-like state. Some healers like for their clients to also be in a sort of altered state, so doing the healing statement will not work, because speaking out loud tends to bring them back to waking conscious awareness. As healers, you will find you can easily go back and forth fairly easily being waking consciousness and an altered state, but the general public may not have this skill. I recommend trying doing the healings on volunteers first, and try various methods before settling in on your preferred method. Try to see if having the client say the statement out loud feels better or if just doing the work while the client is in Alpha state is better.

I personally find that having the client involved in their own healing tends to yield a better and more long-lasting outcome. Awareness is the key to permanent healing. If a person is angry but they don't really know why, finding out they inherited the tendency toward anger from their mother who could not express her anger properly so passed it on to her children goes a long way for a client to feel less inclined to lose her temper so often. On the other hand, some find after a session they just don't have a tendency to lose their cool and things that used to set them off no longer do.

There is a lot to be said about being witness to the healing. Having the client aware of where you are seeing the intrusions, what you are sensing and what you are doing seems to go a long way in solidifying the healing session.

There are certain healing modalities that create a sort of meditative space for the client and then let the Guides loose on the client with no real interaction from the healer. I don't find these healing experiences particularly effective. In certain Reiki circles, I find the healers talking amongst themselves and not even particularly focused on what is happening. Their understanding is that the healer is simply creating the space for the Reiki or the Guides to do the work. However, I believe our active participation is necessary for any healing to work. Even if we are not the ones doing the healing, we have to be an active participant. We have to be present and be witnessing what is happening. We are allowing the Guides to do the healing work by using our body, our mind, and our awareness. If our awareness is planning where we are going out to eat after this is over, the healing is going to be less than effective.

Remember that what we are doing is shifting energy. Energy moves about. It is our intention and our connection with our Healing Team that creates the movement.

I find breath work to be extremely effective as a healing tool. Before onset of the pandemic, I would often use my breath to blow healing into the client, blow pieces of the client's soul back into the body, and I was sad when I had to replace this technique while the pandemic was in full swing.

Use your breath as you feel comfortable and keeping your client's comfort level also in mind. I have even used my breath when doing healings over the phone and various video platforms.

You may also find trapped emotions in locations, in the land, in objects, and all kinds of surprising places. If a bride lost her husband, for example, her grief may be in her wedding band. It may be lodged in the clothing she was wearing at the time, in the room where she was when she learned of the loss, or in the car if she was in a vehicle. It could even be in the home they shared together, even if she chose to move from the location. You can remove trapped emotions from locations and objects using the pendulum or other healing methods. Remember to use your visualization to locate the emotion, be witness to the event, and then release it with love to the Light. Ask your Angels and Healing Team to assist.

n subsequent chapters we will discuss how emotions become beliefs when felt recurrently and more about how cords attach from us to people with whom we have strong emotions.

Suggested Exercises for Chapter Sixteen

Begin with yourself. Identify an emotion that is not serving you. Using one or more of the techniques suggested here, go into an Alpha state. Connect with your guides and angels. Try to discern if the trapped emotion is from this lifetime, another lifetime, or an inherited unhealed emotion from an ancestor. If you cannot discern, then remove the emotion from all three aspects of your soul, using one or more of the suggested techniques.

If you have a partner or someone who will allow you to practice on them, go into their energy field and see if you can identify a trapped emotion and where it is lodged in their body. Use one or more of the suggested techniques and heal, resolve or remove the emotion.

I normally ask my clients how they are feeling after a healing. Sometimes they feel a shift and sometimes they don't. Remember you don't want them feeling worse! If they feel out of sorts or if they are experiencing difficult emotions, ask the Angels and Guides to do any necessary adjustments.

Journal about how you feel after doing the healing on yourself. Follow up with your partner and get some feedback about how they are doing and feeling after the session.

Practice as often as you can and record the experience and any results you are able to verify.

*The Emotion Code by Dr. Bradley Nelson copyright by St. Martin's Essentials; Illustrated edition (May 7, 2019)

(There are multiple sources and copyright editions of this book)

Here is the link on Amazon

https://www.amazon.com/Emotion-Code-Emotions-Abundant-Happiness/dp/1250214505

CHAPTER SEVENTEEN
THOUGHTS AND BELIEFS

I am often asked, "Do emotions come first, or thoughts?"

That is kind of like asking, "Which came first, the chicken or the egg?"

My answer to that is, "It depends."

If I am driving along in a car, and suddenly, without warning, a deer runs out in front of me and I can't avoid hitting the deer, even though I veer sideways off onto the shoulder, the emotion probably came first. The emotion of shock, panic, guilt, anger, or fear shot into me like a bolt of lightning. I had no time to assess the situation or create a thought. I reacted without any thought whatsoever. Thoughts came later.

On the other hand, if I have a sister who once hit a deer while driving down a particular road, and she is consistently warning me that deer are rampant on that area of the road, so I find yourself looking around consistently when driving along that particular route, then the thought came first. It was planted in my head by my sister. I adopted her thoughts and beliefs and emotions about deer and the probability of hitting a deer while driving on a particular road.

A thought becomes a belief when we find ourselves thinking it over and over. The emotions empower the thoughts and beliefs. If my sister is consistently warning me to look for deer while driving on a particular road but I recognize that it is her fear and her limiting belief that "if you are driving on that road, you are likely to hit a deer," and I don't adopt the emotions and beliefs because I recognize that they are not mine, then I won't be affected.

By the way, my sister has never hit a deer as far as I am aware. This was just an example.

Sometimes we find beliefs lodged in our energy bodies that are not ours or that we came into life with. However, when faced with some sort of trigger, we react based on that belief, or we may find we hold that belief as truth even though we are not sure why.

We adopt beliefs from others from various sources.

The most common source is from our parents, significant people in our lives or ancestors. Some beliefs are so engrained in our ancestors that they are just assumed to be true. Our belief often creates the illusion of truth.

When I was married to my first husband, my in-laws were from the mountains of West Virginia. Inherent in their beliefs were many country superstitions. They always planted their gardens under specific moons or signs. I was not allowed to participate in the gardening if I was in my "moon time." (This sometimes proved to be advantageous for me if I didn't feel like participating.) When I was pregnant with my daughter, I was not allowed to go see a popular movie at the time about a child born with a deformity because of the chance of "marking" the child. There were many other beliefs that framed their way of life. Most of these were fairly harmless, but they had stories to prove the validity of their beliefs. It seemed the universe conspired with them to prove the truth of those beliefs. We can all look around us and see how many beliefs are inherited.

We inherit beliefs also from our associations. If we are joined to a belief system, a club or organization, a political party, a culture, or a society, even a gender or a race, we may find the beliefs of that organization affect us.

Finish this sentence.

"You just can't trust...."

What immediately came to mind?

Depending on what associations you have, you will finish the sentence in that manner. If you are a female who consistently ends up in relationships with untrustworthy men, or you associate with a lot of females who have had bad relationships, you may finish this sentence with "men."

If you are a Democrat, you may finish it with "Republicans"

If you are a Catholic, you may finish it with "Evangelicals" or vice versa.

If you are white, you may finish it with "blacks." Or vice versa.

Any thought you think over and over becomes a belief.

All beliefs are up for reconsideration.

Beliefs can be sneaky. They can hide behind every nook and cranny. They can seem logical. They can even seem beneficial.

Here are some sneaky limiting beliefs.

"I have to work hard for my money."

"People who don't work for what they get don't appreciate it."

"Other people's needs are more important than mine."

"I can't.... (fill in the blank.)"

"I should.... (fill in the blank.)"

"No one can love me."

"It is unfair that.... (fill in the blank.)"

"People can't be trusted."

It is my practice to say that I don't necessarily completely align myself with any particular belief system. I find that almost all of

174

them have some sort of merit, but also, almost all of them have margins of error. We are all human. We are all flawed. All beliefs systems have areas where the truth is cloaked in a limiting belief.

Being raised Pentecostal, there were a lot of beliefs that I had to eliminate when I began to expand my awareness. Here are a couple.

"If I don't tithe my money will be cursed."

"If I receive messages outside of the umbrella of Christianity, I am speaking with the devil or his demons."

"It is ungodly to expect payment for spiritual services." (Although this belief apparently doesn't include pastors, evangelists, or other people who make a living doing spiritual work.)

I don't have a lot of accolades after my name. I use a variety of tools in my tool belt. I don't like to label myself. Even though on my website I say that I am a Shamanic Reiki healer, I don't completely align myself with either of those names. I hesitate joining organizations where I have to say I agree to a list of principles and rules.

Alignment with a particular group puts you in the position of having an energetic cord attached to you that can make you an enforcer or advocate of a particular belief.

No matter how long you do belief work, I have found that there are always more beliefs that seem to either sneak back in or hide or reoccur in some way. No matter how many times I think I am healed, every now and again some old belief will poke its head out at inconvenient moments.

While I was writing this healing manual, I reinjured my left knee. At first it seemed I had just overdone it while exercising. I did belief work. I allowed myself to be hypnotized. I had a friend who does Shamanic healing work on me. I worked on myself. My daughter even did a spell. I also allowed my doctor to give me an injection of cortisone.

My immediate thought was, "how can I be writing a healing manual if I can't even heal myself?"

I had forgotten one of the rules that I myself had written in this very manual.

You cannot be attached to an outcome!

The end result is that I stopped writing for almost an entire month.

I was limiting myself! I believed that a healer has to be totally 100 percent healthy!

Limiting beliefs are sneaky! I had totally forgotten that I have never been successful healing my eyesight or other old injuries. And I had forgotten that sometimes people don't get better.

Even healers sometimes cannot heal certain things.

During this time of seeing other healers, I uncovered some old unhealed emotions and beliefs that I thought I had healed. I released some judgements. I forgave some people who wounded me. Who knew?

Healing is a work in progress.

During my little hiatus I also honed some skills and became even more adept at scanning my client's energy fields. My skills improved, even though I have been doing this a long time and I am writing this book!

I share this to say that we may never uncover ALL of our or our clients' hidden emotions or limiting beliefs. Maybe we will. That statement in itself may be a limiting belief!

And we will always be learning, growing and improving our skills.

We are here in the Earth realm to learn, grow, evolve and in the process bring other people more into alignment with their own highest good. If bringing them healing brings them into alignment with their highest good, then we have done our job. If the inner transformation results in a physical healing, wonderful. If not, we can always say that we have done the best we could.

We can never guarantee what the outcome will be in a healing session.

Belief work is a learning curve. It takes intuitive skills to uncover some of the beliefs that hide in a person's energy field. It takes practice and trust in your intuitive abilities to become aware of a hidden belief, to see where it is attached in the energy field and where or who it is corded to.

Let me just add a little addendum here and say that some things may seem to be a limiting belief but are not!

Let's take the issue of trust. Earlier I had you finish the statement, "you just can't trust…"

If you finish the sentence… "You just can't trust.." with something like "men" or "women" then this is obviously a limiting belief.

However, to me, trust is not something freely given. Trust is earned.

I had a client recently tell me in her search for the perfect lover often she is accused of having trust issues. My response to that is that trust is earned, not freely given. You can't possibly trust someone you do not know, or at least you shouldn't. The very accusation that she has trust issues would have been a red flag to me and a sign to definitely not trust them!

Don't take on other people's issues or allow yourself to be manipulated! Not every limiting belief is yours (or your clients!) This takes time and awareness, and a good dose of guidance from your Spirit Communicators.

Suggested Exercise for Chapter Seventeen

Exercise: Uncovering Limiting Beliefs

Keep a notebook or small pad of paper near you or create a note on your phone.

As you go through your day, write down any beliefs you become aware of which are limiting. You will catch yourself saying or thinking them or you will hear other people say them. Anything that is less than empowering is limiting!

When you become aware of a limiting belief within yourself, decide to release it!

Say, "I now release with Love the limiting belief that.... (Fill in the blank.) I release it from this lifetime, from any other lifetime or dimension, and from anything I may have inherited up to seven generations back. It is also released up to seven generations forward. I am free and my children are free. It is done."

Make sure you journal about limiting beliefs and write down as many as you can think of or that you become aware of. The more aware you are when they show up, the easier it will be to recognize them in others.

CHAPTER EIGHTEEN
CUTTING CORDS

We are beings of energy. Energy is the force that gives life to everything that has form. The Creative Force that runs through all things that has no form creates the form in all created things. Whether you believe in a Divine Being who created all things or whether it feels better for you to think of that Life Force as just a Force of Energy doesn't matter.

Everything that exists at some point creates some form of awareness.

All that I have shared so far has to do with shifting energy, or taking whatever issue we are dealing with and shifting it in a way that is more in line with a sense of well-being.

What is commonly referred to as "cords" are energetic links between you and someone else or between you and something else. Some people call them "soul ties" and various other things, but the idea is that there is a "cord" of energy that connects you to something or someone outside of yourself.

We create cords every day. When we think a thought about another person, place, or thing, a cord or strand of energy is connecting you to the object of your thought. Sometimes the thought is just a passing thought, like, "What am I going to have for dinner?" In this case you are creating a cord of thought to the object of some sort of food item. You may say, "Is it tacos? Is it salad? Is it steak? Is it pizza?" You are pulling from a menu in your brain and scanning over the menu to decide what feels good to you. At some point you are going to create a hook into a food item, probably based on a meal you enjoyed in the past, and decide you want to experience that again. You have created a cord to the future and hooked into an item of food you desire. You are probably not going to have a desire for a food item in which you have a prejudice. If you are vegan, you are probably not going to hook into a desire for a steak. You are also probably not going to hook in to an item you have no familiarity with, unless someone has planted a thought in your head about some new food that has some sort of desirable quality.

Once you have decided on a food item and taken the necessary steps to fulfill that desire, the cord will probably go away on its own. But let's say that you really wanted some food in particular but the person who you share your life with did not want the same thing. You put aside your desire and ate what the other person wanted. You most likely still have that latent desire for that particular food item that will only go away if you talk yourself out of wanting it or if you eventually decide to eat it.

This is a simple example of creating an energetic cord between you and the object of your desire.

Cords of energy can be created by thinking of something or someone and then attaching some sort of emotion to the thought. The cords get bigger and stronger the more often we think of and create emotion about a certain target.

Because of the eternal nature of our souls, we can have cords of energy that have been attached a long time, and we may have forgotten or been unaware of their presence. The original cord could have been created before we were born. We could have inherited it. It could have been created in an alternate lifetime on Earth or even somewhere else. It could have been created in between lifetimes.

It is important to note that cords of energy can go both ways. They can go from you to the object of your thought or emotion or they can originate when someone else is thinking or feeling something about you. Cords of energy that originate in other lifetimes or are inherited from the ancestry or a connection to a belief system, a gender, a race, or a myriad of other possibilities, can and do run back and forth without your conscious knowledge or consent.

Cords of energy can be created through some sort of contractual agreement, like a marriage or even a business arrangement. They can be created through religious beliefs. They can be created when you are walking through the grocery store and someone unconsciously senses your energy and creates a link to you. Earthbound souls can create a link to you in order to feed off of your energy.

In today's world cords are often created through the internet and social media. Many people seem almost obsessed with their virtual friendships, with how many people like or share their posts, and with those who have some version of fame. If you are one of those people who cry at movies or become easily triggered emotionally, you are a prime target for a cord becoming attached based on an emotion.

When I was young, I was chronically depressed. I loved to listen to sad songs on the radio, watch sad movies or read books where the main character died of some sort of tragedy or illness. I think the cord may have been created early on in my life, possibly even before I was born. When my mother was pregnant with me, my grandmother passed, who my mother loved deeply. I am sure she felt grief, and the emotion followed me throughout my childhood until well into adulthood.

Many years later I saw my grandmother while in a trance state who I believe had an energetic cord attached to me from before my birth. Even though I am sure she had passed over into the Light there was a cord of energy still attached.

We can have cords of energy that are there through our love for someone or something or their love for us, and that is okay as long as the feelings are mutual. Mutual love is not always the case.

Often, we allow cords to remain intact long after it is healthy to do so based on some distorted sense of love which is really not love at all but another emotion, like desperation or even loyalty. We are desperate or someone else is desperate for a particular relationship which is not reciprocated but we are insistent on having these cords intact. We may feel some sense of loyalty to someone due to our relationship to them or even an obligation to them. In the end the result is never beneficial for either party.

If you feel a cord is attached to you based on a relationship in which the feelings are not mutual, you can cut the cords. You may find you have to periodically cut them again and again, since the other party is continually feeding their thoughts and emotions toward you without your consent. In this case, I recommend doing a shamanic journey to their soul and telling their soul they have to leave you alone. You may need to have a spirit helper with you to assist in cutting the cords permanently.

Sometimes the emotion is not love but hate.

If you have been wounded by someone, and are constantly feeding that wound with your hatred or disdain for that individual, you are not helping yourself by holding on to your hatred. You are actually feeding a cord to that person. Despite your attempts to heal or leave the situation behind, you are actually tied to that person through your judgements and emotions.

As you can see, cords can be created in a myriad of different ways.

Because I have books and videos and blogs out in the public, I periodically have to cut cords to people I don't know! If someone has an emotional response to something I have put out there in to the public, a cord can be created between me and my public.

I also have had the experience of being woken from my sleep based on something that is happening to my clients, or I have had clients become aware when something is going on with me. I have cut cords to clients or students only to have those people email or text me within minutes asking me what is wrong or did they do something to offend me! Several times when I cut the cords these clients became angry and cut ties with me.

It is not healthy for me or you to have these kinds of relationships! Some people in "woo woo world" think it is okay to have this kind of intuition, to know everything someone else is feeling or thinking, but this is not okay with me! I don't want my clients to be so in tune with me that they know when I am having a bad day and I don't necessarily want to know when they are!

One time I awoke in a panic from a dream in which someone was shouting at me: "tell them I am good not bad... tell them I am good not bad!"

In the dream, I became unable to breathe and my heart was racing out of my chest. After I woke up, I was unable to slow my heart rate and go back to sleep. I felt the experience was related to a particular regular client but I went to the doctor anyway because my blood pressure was concerning me. I could not get it back down!

I had a session with that client scheduled for a few days later but she did not show up for her appointment. I was convinced it had to do with her and cut the cords. I actually felt she would probably never contact me again based on my past experience with cutting cords with clients.

A couple of months later she did reschedule her reading and I learned she had experienced a mental breakdown at the very same time I had the dream, possibly the same night. She had been placed in a mental facility having panic attacks and being physically restrained. She reported she was unable to breathe and had in fact screamed a version of the words I heard in the dream, if not word for word. She had missed her appointment because she was restrained and in the hospital.

Listen. I can't be running to the doctor every time a client has an episode. The doctor found nothing wrong with me (of course he didn't) and I did not share that I believed it was a cord attached from a client. (Of course I didn't!) If I had shared, he may have recommended I spend some time in a mental facility!

It is obviously not necessary to share with those who don't understand energy.

So how do you cut cords?

It is fairly easy!

In a previous chapter we discussed scanning a person's energy field and you will need to do that.

First, connect with your Highest Source until you know you are connected.

Imagine yourself going in to your own or your client's energy field (with permission of course!)

You may "see" through your intuitive sight the actual cord and where it is attached. You may sense it using one or more of your other intuitive senses. You may "feel" it in their energy field. You may feel resistance or an energetic intrusion. You may sense or receive information about the source of the cord.

Sometimes the cord is attached to a person. This person is likely someone who is corded due to some sort of thought or emotional connection. It could be a known or unknown ancestor. It could be someone from some other lifetime or even an earthbound spirit.

Sometimes the cord is attached to an emotion, as I previously shared about my experience with grief. I also shared previously a story of how an emotion can be attached in a person's energy field through an ancestor and in different parts of the body. You may find numerous cords.

After you have located the cord, I like to first surround the cord with Divine Light and Love to use as a sort of anesthesia to the cutting process. I visualize a cutting instrument. It could be scissors, a knife, a sword, or even a chain saw! I cut the cord on both ends and send it to the Light. I do not send back to the other person. This is not beneficial for them either!

It is important to be guided by the Divine Presence or your Healing Team when doing this work, as always. They may have you use different methods for cutting the cord.

Sometimes the cord dissolves on its own when touched by the Divine Light or Healing Presence. Sometimes it melts. Each time I cut a cord it feels different and I may use a different method depending on what the Guides direct.

There are times when the cord contains some of the life essence or soul of either the client or the other person, if it is a person. Sometimes difficult emotions or beliefs contain some of the client's life force. It is important you scan the cord to make sure before you cut it or dissolve it. If you don't and the client's life force was inside the cord, the client may not feel better after. They may feel disconnected or lost.

There can be cords attached to the past or future. This is a little tricky since the past and future are not tangible. The past is a little more tangible because the cord is probably attached to a memory and memories can be accessed. When a cord is attached to the future it is usually related to a desire for something to happen in the future and the future never comes, or perhaps to a fear of something happening in the future which the client does not want. In order to bring something you desire into your present moment experience, you have to cut the cord to the future and bring your desire in to the present moment. You can cut cords to the past and the future and bring the client back in to their current physical experience. Make sure you are coating the experience with the energy of Divine Love and Light for the good of all concerned.

It is not possible or even beneficial to cut ALL cords. There are beneficial cords and not so beneficial cords.

Every time you connect with Spirit you are creating a cord of energy between you and Spirit. When you connect with a client you are creating a cord. After a session with a client, it is beneficial to cut the cord, but as I have explained, sometimes a cord reattaches without your conscious awareness.

If you move your home, it is always beneficial to cut the cord between you and the spirit of the land or the house where you lived. Thank it for its connection to you and the gifts it gave you during your time there, and release it to its next owner. In the same way, it is important to create a cord between you and your new home.

Spiritual tools benefit from being connected to your energy. It is important when you buy a new spiritual tool, that you scan its energy field and see what or who it is connected to and see if you are energetically compatible.

Once I bought a new set of tarot cards and upon opening the box, out came a spirit who did not feel good to me! I sat the deck on my altar for a couple of days, but never felt comfortable using the cards. I eventually gifted them to one of my students, who loves them. This does not mean I believe every set of tarot cards has its own spirit or that tarot cards are bad. I use them all the time and have about twenty different decks. This was the only time I ever sensed an incompatible spirit attached to tarot cards. I do believe each set has its own sort of awareness and even if the cards are identical, some of them seem to give me more specific and evidential answers than another deck. However, when I buy a new deck, I always hold them and tune in to see if they are willing to work with me and then if they are, I create a cord of energy between us for the highest good of all.

I recently heard about a student of mine who had a concerning experience in her place of employment. One of her coworkers brought in some crystals which were in the form of obelisks. This is a very ancient symbol and many use these with beneficial results, but in her case, the experience was not pleasant at all.

Within minutes, the store where she worked began to experience angry customers and customers returning items with great angst and emotion. She began to intuit that it was the presence of the obelisks that had created the disturbance in the energy field of the store. When the obelisks were removed, the angry customers and the merchandise returns stopped.

No matter what the opinions are concerning the meaning and use of obelisks, she found it to be a disturbing experience and only found relief when the obelisks were removed. There was obviously a cord of energy between the obelisks and the emotion of anger which created havoc in her store.

Fear is also an emotion which creates cords of energy to undesirable experiences. Fear is one of those emotions that dominates much of society. It has been discovered centuries ago that the easiest way to control the masses is through fear. Any conspiracy theories or beliefs or dogma that exist do so on the premise that you can easily control people if you make them afraid. You can look at almost any horrific event in our history and find a link to mass fear. The whole concept of the devil is a way to make people afraid and to easily control their behavior.

As you can see, the tool of cord cutting is a powerful one that can completely shift a person's experience of life. It is important to cut cords with the assistance of your Healing Team so that you do it within the framework of the client's best interests and their soul contract. If you cut the wrong cord at the wrong time, you could seriously shift a person's experience of life with great consequences.

We as healers have to remember that we are here to bring ourselves and our clients to a place of alignment with their highest good. Perhaps you see a cord but your Guides instruct you to leave it alone. Do it! It may be the case the cord needs to be there for the time being until something else gets resolved. Maybe the client isn't ready to have it cut. Maybe it is benefitting them in some way.

Always approach cord cutting as in all of the tools used in this book with reverence and a working relationship with your Healing Guides or Team. Just because you see something doesn't mean you need to address it.

Healing is a process and is rarely achieved instantaneously, although I don't discount the possibility. If we could achieve instant enlightenment, then what is the point of being here? Being human is being flawed, and vulnerable and wonderful. It is all a delightful adventure!

Suggested Exercises for Chapter Eighteen

You will need a partner for this exercise. It is possible to cut cords from your own energy field, but only if you notice a disturbance or energy drain. When you work on yourself or someone you are close to, you have your own emotions and perspective that often interfere with a healing session. For practice, it is better to work with a partner.

Get into a bit of an altered state of awareness and begin to scan your partner's energy field. You are looking specifically for cords of energy that seem to be linked to other people, times, locations, or things. If the cords seem unhealthy, then ask your Healing Team if it would be beneficial to cut the cord.

Make sure you heal the location where the cord was attached after you cut it. I always seal the location with Divine Love and Light. I send love to the source of the cord but create a boundary forbidding any reattachment.

Most of the time, you don't go looking for cords. During a healing session or perhaps just living life, you will become aware of a cord. Using whatever tools you feel led to use at the time, cut the cord and heal the wound.

CHAPTER NINETEEN
SOME POPULAR HEALING MODALITIES I LIKE AND USE

Reiki

I have mentioned Reiki several times and it is probably the most well-known form of energy healing these days. Most people are somewhat familiar with the healing modality that is now one hundred years old! Master Usui in Japan was given the energy of Reiki in 1922. According to the tradition, Master Usui was meditating on top of a mountain in Japan when suddenly he had some sort of spiritual experience and the ability to heal was placed in his body. He began sharing it and passing the ability on to others through what are called "attunements" and eventually it was spread across the globe. Reiki is a Japanese word that means Universal Life Force Energy. It is collecting the Divine Healing Power into your body and then sending it out to others through your hands, eyes, or intentions.

The healing force is transmitted from teacher to student. Depending on which tradition you align yourself with, you will receive instruction in the art of the laying on of hands, or even transmitting healing energy through your eyes, your feet, and even your heart and mind, and is not limited by time or space. Reiki is normally divided into three levels. Once you reach the third level, you are considered a Master and can attune others and teach classes.

One hundred years have passed since Master Usui received the ability to heal and now there are over 1200 forms of Reiki. It has grown and evolved and now is a form of healing that is practiced in many hospitals, addiction treatment centers, and other alternative healing facilities all over the world.

t is also highly regulated. Here in my home state of Virginia, you must have a massage therapy license or a "fortune teller license" to practice Reiki. I am not sure how much this is enforced. I am sure it is different in various parts of the state. In my hometown, Reiki is offered as an alternative healing option at the hospital. If you have been certified in Reiki, you can volunteer to offer Reiki to hospital and cancer patients. It is strictly volunteer. I am sure the volunteers are not required to have licenses but they are not being paid for their services, either. Bottom line: if you want to practice Reiki or any other form of alternative healing, you must abide by the laws in your area.

I am a Reiki Master Teacher in both the Usui and the Holy Fire® systems of Reiki. All I really have to say about all the different forms of Reiki is that you as an individual need to look within yourself to align yourself with a teacher who resonates with you. I received my "attunements" (now sometimes called placements or ignitions) from three different teachers and each of them felt different to me.

The Holy Fire® is a part of the International Center for Reiki training that is probably the biggest and most well-recognized branch of the Reiki tradition. The president and main facilitator, William Rand, has done extensive research and meditation on his form of Reiki, or what he says was given to him from a channeled message from his spiritual advisor.

You can find him at www.Reiki.org.

If you decide to become a certified Reiki master through his organization, you have to follow an extensive list of rules and agree to only teach and do healings within his guidelines. For this reason, I am not certified through him but am an affiliate Reiki master teacher. I understand his reasonings. If I had my name attached to a form of healing, I would want people who did healings in my name to do them the way I taught.

I am not certifying you to do anything my way. I am teaching you what I know, and hopefully inspiring you to follow your own personal path of healing. This compilation of various healing techniques is for you to use in a way that is resonate with your own soul, and hopefully you will never claim to be doing a Joy Andreasen healing session.

I do find the energy of Reiki to be powerful and healing, especially when combined with some of the other techniques laid out in this book. I highly recommend the experience for your journey of healing.

Radiance Healing Light

Probably over ten years ago, I was introduced to an intuitive healer and teacher named Christen McCormack who founded "Spirit School" in my area. Although I did not go through her whole course of study, on occasion she would have gatherings and various classes which I found to be extremely educational and informative. She was a spiritual intuitive, and has been doing intuitive readings for many years.

Over the course of time, she was channeling her Guides and they gave her a spiritual healing technique called *Radiance Healing Light*.

I could never hope to do it justice, but it is a form of healing which combines the energies of Divine Love, Divine Light, Divine Healing Light and Mother Earth energies into a stream of energy which focuses its power like a laser beam to heal the trapped emotions and limiting beliefs that affect our quality of life. She introduced me to the idea of a healing team, and gave extensive instruction and charts containing various limiting beliefs, trapped emotions and fears that become stuck in our bodies and energy fields.

She teaches a series of classes from beginner to advanced on using the healing technique and incorporating it into your own healing practice. You can become certified using her method, although I have not taken that course of action. I highly recommend these series of classes.

After completing the first course, I was scheduled to teach a Reiki 1 class. I decided to combine the Radiance Healing Light frequency with the Reiki frequency when doing the attunements for my students and I was amazed at the difference in the transmission of the frequency into the energy fields of my students. My students reported a huge transmission of energy that was so strong, many of them needed to sleep the entire next day. One of my students slept for several days. Now I almost give a warning that my Reiki students may need a day of rest after an attunement, so that they can really incorporate the energy in their body.

As of the writing of this book, Christen is writing a book on the technique.

You can learn more about Christen and her technique at www.ChristenMcCormack.com.

Theta Healing®

Theta Healing® is relatively new to me. I was in conversation one day with a fellow healer who asked me if I had ever heard of it, and I had not.

Always interested in various healing techniques, I found that the author and creator of Theta Healing®, Vianna Stibal, had written a couple of books on the technique and offered certification classes on her method.

I ordered her books on Amazon and was immediately hooked!

She had detailed descriptions and instruction on her methods as well as a ton of very valuable information and perspectives! Bottom line, I love this method of healing!

In her method, before performing a healing on anyone, you travel to the seventh plane of existence and connect with the Creator of All That Is before doing the healing. The Creator is the author and perfector of every healing modality and everything that is, both that is the healer and that which needs to be healed.

I mentioned before that sometimes the Guides do not agree with one another on the best course of action. Her method seems to offer a solution to that, as well as to a lot of the other issues that often come up in a healing session.

Just by reading the books I found my sessions with clients became much clearer and more accurate. I still incorporate many of the previously described methods, but Vianna has alternate ways to deal with many of the issues that I cover here. Some of them are a bit shorter than the ways I often heal.

I did ask my Higher Guidance system what their thoughts were and they told me that the Creator is the one who created all of the other forms of healing! Of course they were on board! They did go a step further and say that the Creator of All That Is can be reached at any time and any place, since That Presence is everywhere! I originally found it tedious going through all the steps she describes for reaching that Presence, however sometimes it is a valuable exercise. She even says it is not always necessary to go through all the steps, but in the beginning, it is recommended.

I will say I have not taken her classes but I find the books to be extremely valuable and a priceless tool for any healer!

There are numerous books on Theta Healing® by Vianna Stibal. As far as I know they are all available on Amazon.

www.thetahealing.com

CHAPTER TWENTY

HEALING FOR LAND, HOUSES, THE DEAD OR NON-HUMAN ENERGY FORMS.

In the section on Shamanic Healing techniques, I described the Shamanic way of crossing over souls or clearing energy. I described the White Table and the Rainbow Bridge, which are both valuable tools for clearing souls and helping them to the light.

In the chapter on the use of a pendulum, I described how to do house clearings using a pendulum. I will not repeat that information here. However I do want to focus on some personal viewpoints I have about hauntings.

These days it is almost an obsession to go into haunted houses or locations where tragic events or practices have occurred in hopes of having some sort of experience.

There are countless television shows and events you can pay to attend with the promise of possibly experiencing some sort of paranormal activity.

Here is a truth.

What you focus on grows.

If there is a lot of attention placed on hauntings, ghosts, demons, and paranormal activity, the spirits will not disappoint you.

However, is this beneficial to either the living or the dead?

I am not one of those mediums or healers who particularly enjoys going to events where there may be some sort of haunting. I accept requests to clear homes or locations with great hesitation.

It is not necessarily that I don't like to do it or I don't believe locations are really haunted. On the contrary. I often feel that the practice has been too publicized and people have become too quick to assume that every bump in the night or every unexplained scratch is a ghost.

It is possible to summon the dead from their place of rest and peace and bring them or some piece of their awareness back to an event from their lifetime. If the location happened to be a hospital or a prison, it is likely that this was not their greatest moment. It probably was extremely traumatic to them. It is entirely disrespectful of the dead to expect their worst moments to entertain us.

On the other hand, yes, it is possible they did not go to the light, and in that case, I am available to help them get there.

Believe it or not, some paranormal investigators do not want the dead to find peace. They may be benefitting in some way from the haunting. They may be making money by charging people to experience activity.

This is so wrong.

Once I had a couple that were hoping to be released from their lease by claiming that their home was haunted.

A lot of people watch the television shows and begin to believe their house is haunted every time the house settles or the floor creaks.

Here is another truth.

We are all surrounded by our Angels, Guides, and loving ancestors. Sometimes the elementals hang around. There is a lot of activity in the surrounding field of energy that we cannot see. Much of it is far from scary or harmful.

If you see a woman figure hanging over your baby's crib, it is most likely a grandmother or relative on the other side. If your car keys keep getting moved, it is most likely an elemental. There are numerous possibilities besides some poor ghost or a demon.

However, there are ways to help the dead or other non-beneficial energy sources find peace or resolution.

I often use the energy of the Creator of All That Is, or Source Energy, and the Angels.

If you find yourself at a location that seems to have some sort of disturbing energy or concerning activity, or if you are interacting with a living human who is exhibiting disturbing behavior, you can utilize the Benevolent Forces to assist you.

The first thing to remember is that you do not need to be afraid of these energies. Fear is the food of the heavy energy.

I always call the Angels of Light to assist me when dealing with souls who have not crossed over or forces of harm.

If there is a tremendous amount of harmful or low vibrational activity in a location, there is a likelihood that some unhealed or malevolent energy has gained a foothold there. Drug use, sexual misconduct, theft in all its forms or illegal activity, and of course, suicide or murder can all be influenced by malevolent energy, and can also attract it if it wasn't there already. It is paramount you call upon the Angels of Light to take charge in cases like these.

I like to create a forcefield around me whenever I am going to locations where there may be a nest of difficult emotions or dark energy. This forcefield is made up of the energy of Divine Love and Peace and Joy. Where the Light is, the darkness cannot penetrate.

Remember that it is impossible to rid a location or a person of an infestation of darkness if they want it there. But you can command that it not manifest while you are there.

Once, years ago, I went into a location with my former husband to assist him in doing some carpentry. He had been asked to repair a hole in the wall of a house we had previously rented. Upon entering, we quickly realized that the current residents were avid drinkers. We opened the door to the stench of stale liquor as empty and partially consumed liquor bottles were stacked, dumped, and dispersed throughout the house. At the time, we were very aware of the presence and activity of spirits, and were just learning our authority.

Despite not asking permission from the residents, who likely would have refused, we decided to cast out the spirit of alcohol from the house. As my husband fixed the hole in the wall, I walked around each room and cast out any spirits of alcohol and addiction from the home. We finished our work and left.

The next day, the owner of the house, who was our former landlord, called, flabbergasted.

He reported that when he arrived at the house the next day, the renters had vacated the house in the middle of the night!

Well, at least the hole in the wall was fixed!

These days, I frequently advise clients that they are in charge of their own experience. They can command that the energy of peace, love and joy be all around them and in their home and no other energies that are not compatible with peace, love and joy, are allowed!

I was able to do this successfully in my first marriage when it sometimes became volatile. I would go around to every window and door and command that only peace, love and joy were allowed in the home. My former husband would come home, but immediately leave and go fishing or find something to do outside.

Now I often share this technique with my clients.

One client reported that when she did this, her husband moved out within twenty-four hours!

This doesn't always work. It mostly works when the spouse is abusive or in agreement with dark spirits or nonbeneficial energy. If you just want to get rid of a spouse because you don't love him anymore, this probably won't work. You probably need to empower yourself and make some difficult choices.

When I had a full-time job, I would often declare peace, love and joy into my work space. My boss would sometimes report that as soon as I went to lunch, the phone rang off the hook with complaints. I once received an award from my boss for my ability to deflect angry customers and turn them into happy ones. I highly doubt that this is an award that is bestowed regularly. The happy customer award? It would be nice. But I digress.

The best way to rid locations of non-beneficial energy is to first scan the property using the technique previously described in Chapter 5 on scanning the energy field. You will be able to intuit what energy is in the house and then call on the Angels to assist you in clearing it.

In the case of dark energy that has never inhabited a human form, that energy probably does not necessarily want to go to the Light. I normally call on the Angels to cast a net of Light and capture any darkness that has intruded on a location or a person without their permission. If they did not ask permission to intrude, then I don't have to ask permission to remove them. I then ask the Angels to capture in the net of Light any energy that is there without the permission of the person or persons involved and take it to the Light to be transformed.

If a person in some way is in agreement with the darkness or it is serving them in some way, the clearing will not last. They want it there! It will come back, or similar energy as what was removed.

Most of the time people don't realize they are in agreement with the darkness. They are mad. They are fighting with someone. They like feeling victimized. They want attention, or sympathy, or *something*.

Yes, I have had the darkness refuse to leave because the person wanted them there! In that case, my job is done. It is up to the person to decide what they want.

Sometimes it is not ghosts or demons or dark conscious energy at all. It is trapped emotions!

Yes! It is possible for someone to experience an intense emotion and for that emotion to seep into a location until it is removed and healed.

Places where car accidents happen frequently seem to become infested with the energy of the crash and the emotions that accompany the crash. Hospitals, jails, mental health facilities, and other locations where difficult emotions happen frequently can become infested. It is possible to clear the locations of the congestion, but if the activity or the emotions continue, it will become re-infected.

I like to clear my hotel rooms or other vacation spots of any congestion before my trip. I once connected to three spirits in a hotel room before a trip. During my trip, I ran in to each of them in turn, although not necessarily in the hotel room. On one occasion, I checked into a hotel room but forgot to clear the energy before my arrival. My dreams that night were filled with numerous spirits coming and going all night.

The process for clearing a person of a spirit is sort of the same as a location. I scan the energy field. I see what or who is there. I call on the Angels of Light to surround the person with a net of Light, pulling out any energy that is not compatible with the client's greatest good, and transport them to the Light. I then call on the

Healing Angels to replace whatever was there with Divine Love and Light and then energy of the light of their soul.

Not everyone wants this to occur! It is important to ask the person if they want to be free before doing this! Yes, I have had people say no!

Sometimes a person's mouth says yes but their soul says no! When someone says yes but when you get in to their energy field there is resistance or the person's soul says no, then you must stop. There is some reason why the soul is saying no and any attempts to rid them of nonbeneficial energy will be unsuccessful.

Remember that every location has its own guardian spirit! It is my practice to contact the spirit of the land first before going in to a location for whatever reason. I like to offer the spirit of the land a gift of some kind. I like to use apples but you can use whatever feels good. Native people often used cornmeal or tobacco or sage.

Ridding locations of non-beneficial energy is a lot easier if you have the spirit of the land participating or at least in agreement.

There are a lot of rituals which rid locations of non-beneficial energy. In a previous book I related how I became aware that the land that a church I was attending had been the location of a Native battle and that the blood of Native people was in the land. I was given a ritual to clear the land. I gathered a few people who were in agreement with my assessment or at least trusted the information I had received and we danced in circles around the land, chanting and probably praying in tongues since that was the belief system I was in at the time. We danced around in a circle seven times and released the blood from the land to the light.

Not too long after I did the ritual, I ended up leaving that particular church so I never really found out if any changes happened after the ritual. (Well, I left. So, there was that.) The biggest change happened within me. I discovered that there was a lot more to the spirit world than what I originally thought. My adventures into the world of spirit began to expand in that moment on that land.

It may be an important consideration when clearing land or buildings that you may very well be the one who ends up leaving!

If you are spiritually sensitive, your own personal Higher Guidance system will instruct you on the individual ways you can clear land and/or people and even animals of the energies that seem to create havoc or heaviness.

*One really wonderful book on this subject is *Spirit Releasement Therapy A Technique Manual* by William J Baldwin, DDS, PhD by Headline Books Inc copyright 1992 ISBN 092991516X

I had to take this book slowly and I rarely recommend it just because it is really intense. It took me an entire year to get through this book. When you focus on this type of technique you have to really sandwich it between periods of doing other work.

Spirit releasement from people or land or locations is intense.

If you engage in this activity, make sure you take frequent energetic baths and spend time in the presence of the Creator of All That Is frequently lest you become weighed down from the intensity of this work.

In Holy Fire® Reiki there is another way to do this work without becoming so involved in the intensity. You simply connect with the Holy Fire, or Holy Spirit, or as in Theta® healing, the Creator of All That Is, and allow it to do the work, with you only needing to witness it occurring. That way you are an observer, but not necessarily a participant.

Wrapping yourself up in the energy of Divine Love, Divine Light, and the Creative Force energy will keep you safe and protected. However, if you become ill or begin feeling weighed down, I recommend an immediate shift away from doing this work and focus on other healing techniques for a while.

Suggested Exercises for Chapter Twenty

When you are out and about, take note of the energy in a location. Scan the energy and see if you sense any unsettled feelings. Using your intuitive senses, note any changes in temperature, any smells that don't have an explanation, any notable sounds, or other variables from your psychic senses.

If you sense a presence that does not feel good, call on the Angels to surround it with a net of Divine Light and escort it to a better place for healing or resolution.

If you have been successful, you should notice a sensation that feels better. The air may seem to be lighter; you may feel a rush of joy come over you; your heart may beat a little faster for a moment or two; or you may generally feel more aligned with a sense of well-being.

Using whatever healing technique you feel comfortable with, from your practice in the exercises from this book or in your studies outside of this information, send healing energy to fill in any gaps from where the presence or energy was located.

Call on Divine Love and Light and Joy to fill the area or the person with high vibrational energy.

It is important to bathe yourself with Divine Light and Love when doing this work and have strong boundaries in place.

CHAPTER TWENTY-ONE
HEALING OR FINISHING
KARMIC PATTERNS

This chapter was kind of an afterthought.

Some spiritual teachers believe and teach that karma is not a real thing. I think it is.

My understanding of karma and the way I am presenting it here in this book is the following.

A familiar statement in science is "For every action there is an equal and opposite reaction."

If you are not necessarily a science buff, you may have heard this saying. "Whatever goes around comes around."

In the Bible, the principle goes like this, "Whatever you sow that shall you also reap." Galatians 6:7.

Generally, karma is the belief in payback. If you are a good person, good will come to you, and if you are a bad person, bad will be repaid to you.

It's the basic law of sowing and reaping.

If you plant green bean seeds, green beans are going to grow. And normally, you get more green beans than the seed you originally placed in the ground.

But here is an addendum. If the ground is not fertile, or the seed does not get enough sunshine or rain, or there are too many rocks in the dirt or for a variety of other reasons, that seed has the potential to grow or it has the potential to die.

204

That is why you don't always get paid back for everything you do or say.

But here is the fertilizer to that green bean seed.

What you focus on grows.

We already talked about emotions, thoughts and beliefs, and they tend to have a lot to do with whether or not your green beans grow.

There have been many studies done to show that plants respond to emotions and that talking to plants and sending them love really does make them grow better. Conversely, if you send mean or hateful thoughts to them, they are also affected.

So, karma seems to be a little like that too.

In numerology, six is the number of karma. You could call it the settling of accounts. One day recently I was contemplating on my year, and thinking about if I could see accounts coming up to be settled. What exactly does that mean?

Anything in your life which has remained unresolved, comes up to be resolved.

Guilt is a common catalyst for the experience of karmic repercussions.

Guilt is different from remorse. Remorse is being sorry for something that you have done that has hurt someone in some way. Guilt is feeling bad in general, maybe for who you are or for what someone else has done or for how your actions affected others.

Guilt is one of those emotions you can inherit. Maybe you feel like it is your job to make up for all the bad in the world. Or maybe all the bad that a relative did. "My father was a drunk, so I will never drink, and I will do everything in my power to fight against the sale of alcohol."

When you are feeling a sense of guilt or remorse for something you have done, or someone else has done, or you just generally feel guilty all the time and try to make up for the sins of humanity, that is a feeble attempt to resolve karma. The problem is, you never quite feel like the debt is paid.

Judgement is another example of karma that never seems to get resolved.

A boy's father is unfaithful to his mother. He judges his father for his infidelity but grows up and is similarly unable to be faithful to his partners.

A girl judges her father for working all of the time and never having time for family and then she grows up and becomes obsessed with her career which takes her away from her family.

Judge not, that you be not judged. Matthew 7:1-3

I find that if I get angry when someone cuts me off in traffic, within five minutes I have done the same to someone else. This may seem insignificant, but it is a good example of the law of sowing and reaping.

None of us who are human can say we have never done anything regrettable. We may be able to make amends in some cases, but most of the time, the infractions happened far in the past and no matter what we do, it never seems like we have done enough to make the guilt go away.

When my daughter was fourteen, I left our church and was subsequently ostracized from the congregation. Her two best friends were no longer allowed to speak to her or have any contact. Two years later, I left her father and caused a significant amount of pain and grief to her and her father. This year she turned thirty-seven and I finally had to admit that I still felt guilty for the affect it had on her life. Every time I did something for her, I had to wonder if I was doing it out of love or out of some sort of attempt to make amends.

This revelation prompted me to realize that we can decide that we have served our sentence at some point and release ourselves from the guilt of our decisions. I realized I had been punishing myself for over twenty years!

I then declared to the Universe that I was closing out any karma related to my decisions and how they affected her. I declared that from that day forward, any choice to do anything for her was done from a place of love, not obligation and not guilt. I no longer needed to pay for my perception of how my decisions affected her.

This is a perfect example of deciding to finish karmic repercussions. We simply need to decide to be done.

A simple statement is normally enough to be done. We can state the intention to the Universe, or to the soul of the person we feel connected to in some karmic way.

I could have said, "Dear daughter, thank you for choosing me for your mother. I have done the best that I could but I have made mistakes. I am now declaring that I have paid for my mistakes and from now on, any time I choose to give to you or to do anything for you, I will be doing it because I love you, not because I feel obligated to pay you back for how my choices affected you or because my skills in mothering were lacking in some way. Our karma is done."

This actually frees our relationship to evolve to the next level! Now we can interact in a healthier way.

You can do a little self-inventory and I am sure you will find examples of this in your own life.

I still believe in making amends. I just don't believe we have to pay for eternity. At some point, the debt is paid in full.

I tend to hesitate to let grievances go if the other person shows no remorse or makes no attempts to make amends. I don't believe that as spiritual people, we are required to let go of grievances. I think we have to take time to process our emotions and decide when we are ready to move on. And that takes as long as it takes.

When we are ready to settle the karma of a specific issue, the first step is acknowledging it. Then we can choose a way that feels good to us to help us release it. For me, a simple statement to the Universe is sufficient. We may want to give to a charity, or do a ritual of some kind, or write the issue on paper which we bury, or burn as a sign of closure.

We can also extend that to cover past lives and things we seem to be paying off for our ancestors.

It takes some intuitive investigation to uncover past life and ancestral karma, but it does affect our lives and at some point, the debt is paid. We do not have to pay forever.

In my sessions with clients, I rely on my Guides to tell me when a client is feeling guilty or if a past karmic issue is holding them back from living their best life. The Guides will give me a ritual to give them or a statement to say to release the karma. Sometimes I am able to cut off the karma with my pendulum or another tool.

Healing works best if the client is aware and involved in the healing work. Yes, sometimes I heal the person's soul without their conscious awareness, if the soul has given permission, and many times that is sufficient. If I am seeing a client and we heal ancestral karma, often the family members also benefit and they probably knew nothing about the session!

Suggested Exercises for Chapter Twenty-One

Take some time to do some internal inventory. Can you see patterns that seem to be karmic in nature?

Think about something that is occurring in your life, and try to look into the past and see if any memories are triggered about a similar issue which may be repeating over and over. Once the father of a client stole car parts and sold them as a teenager and never could seem to own cars that did not break down. The daughter ended up having similar issues with cars until we broke the karma being passed down from her father.

Can you think of similar issues in your life?

This may take some meditation time and connecting with your Guides.

Journal about what comes up for you.

CHAPTER TWENTY TWO
TWO – CO-CREATING WITH NATURE

Entire books and courses are out there exploring using crystals and plants to bring about healing, and I don't consider myself enough of an expert to really explore these tools extensively, but I wanted to include a little bit about healing using these tools.

Mother Earth has gifted us with a myriad of tools which we can utilize to bring about healing and a sense of well-being in our bodies, minds, and souls.

In Shamanism we believe that everything that is created has some form of conscious awareness. It may not be like our version as we live out our lives as humans, but it is there nonetheless.

It is said we could completely heal and sustain ourselves using weeds that spontaneously grow outside in our backyard if we only knew it. Most of the time we mow them down or even spray poison to kill them because they make our lawns look less than pristine.

It is not completely necessary to go online and buy crystals from far away lands or that have created massive holes in the earth where these rare and often expensive crystals and gemstones have been excavated.

Mother Nature gives us everything we really need within easy reach! Many Shamans heal using sticks, stones and plants that they find as they walk through the woods or even in the back yards of their clients!

Most of us are not adept enough at communicating with the plant spirits to instinctively be able to receive direct understanding of the healing properties of plants and so we depend on books and experts to tell us. It is said that the indigenous medicine men are able to directly communicate with the plant spirits and the plants tell them how they are to be used for healing. I am not going to include a list here of beneficial plants and crystals, but you can find multitudes of information online! There are even phone apps which tell you what a particular weed is just by taking a picture of it. I can't compete with that, and would not try!

Most of us who think outside of the traditional mainstream way of thinking enjoy spending time in nature, and somewhere inside of us is the memory that one time long ago we lived in some form of cohabitation and collaboration with the world around us. The world of nature is as dependent on us for their survival as we are of them. We live here on the earth, and we share it with the spirits of nature.

So how can we reestablish a relationship with the spirits of nature?

The first and most important thing to remember is that the spirits of nature deserve respect. We should always treat the earth and land and water with the same respect we would expect and desire.

If I consider removing something from its natural habitat such as a stone or a feather or even a plant, I ask first! I try to always give a gift in return for its agreement to come home with me!

Even when I am at the local nursery or home improvement center buying plants for my home or yard, I always try to tune in to the soul of the plant and ask if it wants to come home with me. Once I get home, I will ask it where it wants to be placed in the yard. I thank the plant for agreeing to join my family and welcome it to my home. I talk to the plants regularly. If one seems sickly or at the end of its life cycle, I thank it for the time it spent with me and ask if there is anything I can do to assist it in either recovering or being comfortable as it transitions.

Once, years ago, I bought a crystal geode while vacationing in Florida. Upon arriving home, after only a day or two, I felt it communicating with me and telling me it wanted to be buried outside in the yard! I was devastated! However, I was sure I was receiving direct communication from the soul of the geode, so I complied.

I marked the place in the yard where it was buried, so I would know if it ever decided it was ready to be dug up, but I surrendered the idea that it may do so. After a couple of years, I sort of forgot about it.

One night during a heavy downpour of rain, my husband and I were relaxing watching television. The rain was coming down particularly hard. Out of the blue, I heard the geode calling to me. It was ready to be dug up now!

It was dark outside and pouring down rain! What! You mean right now????

My husband, although not quite as "woo-woo" as me, was used to these things happening, so he was only a little surprised when I got up from my comfy position on the couch and announced that the geode had told me it wanted to be dug up right now and I had to go do it.

It took me a few minutes to find the place where I had buried it. The marker that I had placed over it had long since been moved. I had to dig a few holes in the ground before I found it. It was dark, rainy, and wet!

I brought it inside where it has happily resided since! Now it holds my pendulums and helps to charge and cleanse them. I sit the geode in front of the window during the full moon or occasionally put it outside overnight, but it is happy and content now.

I can't say that all my stones and crystals communicate so specifically as that one did, but I am happy to know that I did receive the message and was able to follow its requests.

So, what things can we do to reestablish a relationship with the spirits of nature?

The first thing to do is to spend time outside! Take walks. Go outside in your bare feet when the weather is conducive. Give gifts to the spirits of nature on occasion. I like to take an apple, cut it into four parts, and place each part on the four corners of my property. I do this whenever I feel inspired or whenever I have made some sort of request.

There are guardian spirits of particular parcels of land. It is important to establish a working relationship with the guardian spirits.

I always like to address the spirits of the land whenever I am doing any kind of spirit work or even visiting homes or properties. I ask them for permission to be there and thank them for their presence. Even when I perform wedding ceremonies, I like to arrive a little early and ask the blessing of the spirits of the land and the ancestors of the couple who are marrying. I charge the ancestors who are blessing the union to be present and the ones who are opposed to stay on the outside of the property.

There are other ways to gain favor with the spirits of nature.

If you see an animal in distress, try to help!

Recently a bird somehow made its way into our attic. It took my husband and me awhile to figure out what the noise was, but we eventually figured it out. We went outside and took off one of the vents so that the bird had a way of escape, and I called upon an Angel to assist me in leading the bird to the hole to its freedom. It only took about five minutes to gently push the bird in the direction of the open vent hole. Using my awareness, I visualized the attic and the bird. I energetically stood behind the bird with the Angel and we grew the energy field behind him and nudged him toward the open hole.

After the bird flew ecstatically to its freedom, it circled above our house three times before flying away. I took that to be its soul saying thank you.

My husband and I try to assist the wild critters as much as we can. We feed the feral cats who live in our neighborhood. We once rescued a snapping turtle who was attempting to cross a busy intersection. I always say good morning to the crows who cawk at me when I emerge from the house in the morning.

Many times, nature has messages for us but we fail to receive the messages because we aren't paying attention! I always notice which direction birds are flying over my path and how many birds and what kind they are. If I am spending time out in nature, I try to pay attention. I notice which critters show up and how many and where they are located or what they are doing. I greet any animals that show up when I am out on my walks. I thank them for sharing their home with me.

I also make deals with animals that are encroaching on my home. I tell any ants or mice that they are welcome to live outside, but inside is my territory. I give them gifts for leaving or offer them opportunities to leave on their own before taking more drastic measures.

Periodically, I may go outside and place my hands on the ground and send healing energy into the earth. I send a telepathic message to transmit the energy to wherever it is needed. I send healing energy into the water supply, the flowers, the dirt, and whatever comes to mind.

Suggested Exercises for Chapter Twenty-Two

Go outside! Walk around in nature and pay attention! Notice any critters that happen across your path. Take note of the direction they seem to be heading, how many there are, and if there is a message from them to you. Take your awareness closer in to their energy field. Send them love and express gratitude to them. Offer a gift if you happen to have anything with you. If not, you could offer healing energy, love from your heart, or a piece of your hair as an expression of thanks.

If you have any plants, crystals, feathers, or other natural objects which you use in your spiritual work, take some time to connect energetically with those items. See how it feels to be inside of them. Take note of any flashes of insight or messages from the spirit or consciousness of the items. If you feel they want to be relieved of their duties, place them somewhere out in nature and give them back to the environment. Thank them for their service. Be willing to surrender your will to theirs. This is respect!

Do your own research and find the properties of the plants, herbs or crystals that you have in your possession, but don't limit yourself to the established properties. It could be that the items have a different purpose for being in your life.

On occasion, offer gifts to the spirits of nature. Thank them for co-creating life on Earth with you and apologize for any lack of respect you have previously had for them.

CHAPTER TWENTY-THREE
COMBINING HEALING TOOLS

In this book I have spent a good deal of time describing and giving instruction in a variety of healing practices based on the training I have received in various modalities as well as what my own personal Guides have shared with me.

If you have gotten to this point in the book, and have been practicing the various suggested exercises, you are ready to venture forth in taking the various tools and using them in tandem with one another and your own journey of healing.

When you are first getting started, you should gather together friends and family who are willing to allow you to work with them.

Before you begin, it is important to set sacred space. Call in your helping spirits in the way that feels good to you.

To get started, you will need to establish a link with your recipient. Sometimes all you need is to hear the person's voice giving you permission. I often ask the recipient for their birthday, or ask them to say their name out loud three times.

It is often beneficial to ask the recipient what their intention is for the session. This is not completely necessary, because the Guides will normally go in the direction they want to go, and usually cover all that person's wants and needs, but intention is an important aspect of the recipient leaving the session feeling good about the interaction.

I personally find that going to the Creator and linking with that Divine Energy is extremely beneficial and increases my ability to scan a person's energy field and get valid information. I ask the Creator to call in the Highest and Best Spirit Helpers, including my healing team, my power animals, ancestors, and other benevolent spirit helpers. I ask that the recipient's spiritual team also be present and work with my team to bring about the highest and best outcome.

At this point I normally enter the recipient's energy field through their crown chakra. If you desire, you can enter this person's sacred garden, or go into your garden and ask for pertinent information. Be led by your intuition. You may find you prefer one method over another, or that sometimes you are going in to their energy field through the crown, and other times you are going into the sacred garden. Find the method that feels good to you!

Whichever method you choose, at this point you are going to do a scan. Notice any intuitive information that comes through. If you see visuals, note that what you see may be literal or symbolic. If you see, for example, a bicycle, this could be an actual bike, it could relate to a childhood event, it could relate to a number of things. Sometimes it may be not an actual bicycle, but bicycle-like. It could be a motorcycle. It could be a tricycle or a toy with wheels. Try to get closer and see what more information you can receive about the bicycle. First tell them what you are seeing and ask if the bicycle is significant to them. If not, then get closer and find out who or what the bicycle represents. Note if you see the chakra in or close to a particular chakra. A bicycle in the throat chakra could represent asking for a bike as a child and never receiving it where a bike in the base chakra could represent wanting a bike but not being able to afford it, or a bicycle accident, or a traumatic event in childhood possibly related to a bicycle. It could also symbolize moving forward, but not in the fastest way that is available. Use your intuition to receive more information.

If you are not receiving details about what you are sensing, such as the bicycle, use your pendulum and ask questions. Is this bike speaking of a childhood event? Is this bicycle related to a child who wants a bike? Etc. etc.

When you are able to ascertain what spirit is telling you about the bicycle, then you can move on to what needs to be healed.

If you are not able to validate the symbol, then just set it aside for now. Sometimes validation comes later. There is no reason to beat it to death if you can't verify the significance.

Let's say for example your recipient was in a bicycle accident as a child that put them in the hospital.

You are now going to take your awareness to that period of time. Note any emotions or limiting beliefs that seem to present themselves to you based on that event. Some limiting beliefs may be: I am not safe. Bicycles are dangerous. Adults can't be trusted. I am clumsy. Note any emotions that come up. Fear. Anger. Grief. Self-loathing. Pain. Note, if you can, where that emotion or belief seems to be stuck.

At this point you can choose a variety of tools to remove that stuck emotion or belief. You may want to try the different suggested tools in order to remove the emotion or belief. Do it gently and with love. We have already discussed in other chapters how you may want to handle this. There may be a cord to the past that needs to be cut. You may use your pendulum to remove the stuck emotion or perhaps a magnet. You may use Reiki or one of the other suggested healing modalities. You may use a feather or other natural tool. You may lead the recipient in a statement of release.

After you have removed the energetic intrusion, fill the empty space with Divine Love and Light and the light of the recipient's soul. You may use color, or sound to fill in the space.

At this point I like to ask the recipient how they feel. Normally I will feel better if the process is complete and I will know if there is resistance or something is not shifting. When you practice enough, and your link to them is strong, you will feel whether there has been a shift or not. However, asking them keeps them involved in the session. Sometimes they may feel worse so you will have to go deeper and see what has been exposed or damaged and heal that too.

You can continue in the process as long as you feel you are being led to do so by your healing team.

You may see in your inner sight a loved one or acquaintance on the other side. Maybe a childhood friend passed in a bicycle accident. You will need to ascertain if that person is in the light or why they showed up in the session and address that.

Example:

I recently connected to a client's energy field and felt a tingling in the left ear. I understand that the left side is the female side and I felt it had to do with words. I heard the number "3". The client confirmed she had experienced ringing in the left ear and pressure for as long as she could remember. At first, I went back to the age of 3 and it didn't feel exactly right but I could see a grandmother figure extremely close to her ear. She could not remember any specific words her grandmother may have said to her that stuck with her, but she related a tale about her grandmother.

When she was a child, her mother, her sister, and herself were living with her grandmother and grandfather. Her grandfather was a drinker and, at some point, cast them out of the home. The grandmother had allowed it to happen, and did not speak up in their defense.

Three days before my client's seventh birthday, her grandmother committed suicide.

I asked my pendulum if the grandmother had gone to the light, and the pendulum said "no." I asked if the grandmother was attached to my client on the left side close to her ear, and the pendulum said, "yes."

218

At this point, I tuned into the grandmother to see if she had something to say. She said she was never able to speak up for herself or her girls in life, and had attached soon after her passing.

I called in the Angels to separate the earthbound grandmother from her granddaughter and escort her to the Light.

My client reported immediate relief on the left side of her face.

In this example, I entered the client's energy field through her crown chakra and immediately felt tingling in the left ear. I am using my sense of intuitively feeling what the client is feeling. I used my psychic vision to see the grandmother right next to the client's ear. My intuitive hearing said the number "3." I used the pendulum to ask questions I was not receiving information about otherwise. I used my mediumship skills to chat with the grandmother and the Angels to remove her from the client and take her to the light.

Some people mistakenly think that intuitive information comes in dictation form. It does not. Well, I guess sometimes it does, but normally it comes in bits and pieces. It takes a variety of skills in various intuitive abilities as well as skill in various healing modalities and tools to bring forth a healing.

If, for whatever reason, the grandmother would have resisted going to the light, or the client seemed to be having trouble experiencing relief, I could have employed some other tools. I could have used a magnet to remove the grandmother. I could have used my feather or I could have cut the cord between them. It is important to have a variety of skills because sometimes the tried and true and favorite tools may not work in every situation. If a client seems resistant to one tool, they may be inclined to allow another one. Sometimes if someone comes to me expecting a traditional Reiki session, and I don't put them on a table, they will be disappointed. If they come expecting a Shamanic healing session and I don't shake rattles or beat drums, they will resist other healing methods. As soon as I pull out the rattles, I will feel their energy shift.

Having a variety of skills in various healing methods will enhance your work as a healer. You will need time to develop each of these skills to perfection before hanging your shingle as a healer.

Suggested Exercises for Chapter Twenty-Three

Line up some friends or family members to do practice sessions on.

Using a variety of the skills you have been practicing in each of the chapters of this book, or in your own personal studies, go into their energy field and receive information most beneficial for their session. Try to utilize each of the skills you have been practicing and incorporate a variety of tools to bring relief or a sense of well-being.

It is a great idea to take notes after or record your sessions in your journals for future reference. (I personally am really bad about doing this unless I have a client coming to me on a regular basis.)

CONCLUSION FOR NOW

We as healers are here to bring healing to whoever or whatever needs it. We are not the source of the healing. We are channeling the healing energy from Source. We don't get to choose who or what deserves healing. We also don't get to choose the outcome.

We can all be healers in some form or another!

The most important way for us to be healers is through kindness. Assist those in need when it is in your power to do so. However, if someone needs to do something for themselves, don't take the lesson away from them by doing too much.

Always send healing energy with no consideration of a desired outcome. Leave that to the soul of the recipient and Source.

Heal yourself!

The good news is, as you are channeling healing energy out into the world in whatever form, you are also creating healing for yourself. You can't heal others without benefitting yourself.

Don't allow others to shame you into believing that you have to give of yourself freely with no boundaries or exchange of energy. People who want to continuously receive something for nothing have more issues than you can heal by giving them more than what you should or feel led to do. Have some self-restraint. You don't have to and can't possibly heal everyone who needs healing.

You also don't have to be available at everyone's beck and call. You can have business hours. You need time for rest and rejuvenation! Do things for yourself and take frequent breaks!

Don't think that you have to be completely healed to bring healing to others. Life is a work in progress. None of us have completely reached enlightenment, with possibly an exception or two somewhere. I notice clients seem to find me who often have issues similar to my own. Many times, when I am channeling, I receive the message for myself even while communicating it to someone else.

Remember healing is allowing yourself to be aligned with your highest good, spirit, soul and body. Healing is not always getting better. Sometimes we have to surrender our need for a specific outcome. Bringing healing to others is assisting them in aligning with their own sense of well-being. Sometimes people get better and sometimes they don't.

When we heal others, we are providing them an opportunity to heal themselves. We are aligning their energy field and their soul memories with a sense of well-being. Some people do not want to be healed. We can't force healing on anyone.

In the same way, we can't assume someone was not healed because we did not see any sort of change. Healing is sometimes instantaneous, and sometimes gradual.

You may be sowing a seed in their soul that sprouts up in some form at some point in the future.

And you may not get the credit.

It doesn't matter.

Heal anyway.

Do good anyway.

Thanks for reading to the end!! Obviously, there is no end to a healing manual. There is always more to learn.

I may not have covered an area of healing you may feel is important. I am sure there is someone out there who has covered it!!

Feel free to check out what classes, gatherings, and events I have coming up or to schedule a session at www.whispersofjoy.net.

I appreciate you!

DISCLAIMER AND PERSONAL ETHICS

On my website, I have a list of personal ethics and a disclaimer which states that I hold no legal responsibility for the choices that people make in response to the sessions I do for them. In some states it is required that I say my services are "For Entertainment Purposes Only."

I am an ordained minister through the Universal Life Church, but in my state of Virginia, I am also required to obtain a "fortune teller's license." Despite feeling a bit of "yuk" at this description of my services, I do comply with the law in my state. By possessing this license, I am stating that people who come to me understand that I am not responsible for the choices they make as a result of my services and I guarantee no specific outcome.

I hate that this is necessary but it seems in these modern days there is the occasional person who does not want to take responsibility for their own choices in life and wants to blame someone.

I am comfortable saying that the practices and suggestions in this book are for informational, educational and entertainment purposes only.

Here are my personal ethics.

Personal Ethics

I post this on my website, www.whispersofjoy.net, but I repeat here so we are all on the same page and you know where I am coming from.

1. The purpose of my services are to empower, comfort, and guide my clients or offer perspective as an objective third party. I use

divinatory tools, intuitive guidance, and energy shifting rituals that have had the result of a renewed sense of joy and well-being from my clients. I will never advise a client to forgo seeing a professional or to ignore medical diagnosis or to stop taking medication prescribed by a licensed professional.

2. I do not believe our lives are fixed or unchangeable. I believe and always stress to my clients that they are the authors and creators of their own destiny. Any information, advice, or energy healing tools or rituals I may use only enhances a client's sense of personal power and well-being. The client is then responsible for any choices they make after a session.

3. If I can't read the cards or other divinatory tools clearly for a particular client, or feel the information is vague or that I cannot get a good link to the client for an accurate reading, I will tell them.

4. I welcome clients of all religions, cultures, ethnicities, spiritual paths, sexual orientation and gender identity.

5. I try to be as objective, non-judgmental and neutral as possible when giving readings. If I don't agree with a client's choices, I may tell them, but I leave all decisions up to them. No one can claim they will never give advice outside of their own personal perspective. All I can say is, I do the best I can to offer guidance as free of personal opinion and bias as possible.

6. I will not give advice in areas I am not qualified. If a client persists, I may offer guidance based on my perspective, but I will reiterate that I am not qualified to offer assistance and my perspective is offered as an opinion.

7. I will not do a reading for someone under the age of 18 without the parent's consent. Sometimes I find people make appointments and I do not know beforehand what their age is. If this happens and I am made aware of your age, I may not decide to see you.

8. I retain the right to refuse to answer any questions posed by the client that I deem to be unethical or in violation to a person's right to privacy or safety.

9. I reserve the right to refuse my services to anyone at my own discretion.

10. All consultations are confidential unless I feel that a person's well-being or safety are in danger. I reserve the right to notify law enforcement or authorities if I feel a crime has been committed.

11. Refunds for any services provided are at my own discretion. I also retain the right to offer my services at reduced or free prices at my own discretion.

12. I will not charge an exorbitant amount of money to remove a curse, offer a healing, or suggest that the client must agree to come back to me on a continual basis. Although healing is hardly ever a one-time-fix-all situation, the decision to see me on a regular basis or even the frequency of such visits is completely up to the client. My hope and desire is that eventually I will work myself out of a job and the client will not always need me.

Made in the USA
Middletown, DE
04 March 2023

26035591R00126